William Ewart Gladstone

Vaticanism

An answer to reproofs and replies

William Ewart Gladstone

Vaticanism

An answer to reproofs and replies

ISBN/EAN: 9783337244347

Printed in Europe, USA, Canada, Australia, Japan

Cover: Foto ©Lupo / pixelio.de

More available books at **www.hansebooks.com**

AN ANSWER

TO

REPROOFS and REPLIES.

BY THE

RIGHT HON. W. E. GLADSTONE, M.P.

LONDON:
JOHN MURRAY, ALBEMARLE STREET.
1875.

CONTENTS.

		PAGE
I.	INTRODUCTION	5

THE REPLIES WHICH HAVE APPEARED ON THIS OCCASION. THE INSULT. EVIDENCES OF PERSONAL LOYALTY, ALL THAT COULD BE WISHED. DR. NEWMAN. HIS REMARKABLE ADMISSIONS. EVIDENCES AS TO THE CHARACTER AND TENDENCIES OF VATICANISM; MOST UNSATISFACTORY.

II. THE RUSTY TOOLS. THE SYLLABUS 19

    1. WHAT ARE ITS CONTENTS? 21
    2. WHAT IS ITS AUTHORITY? 32

III. THE VATICAN COUNCIL AND THE INFALLIBILITY OF THE POPE 37

BREACH WITH HISTORY, NO. 1. FROM THE OPINIONS AND DECLARATIONS OF THE ROMAN CATHOLICS OF THE UNITED KINGDOM FOR TWO CENTURIES.

IV. THE VATICAN COUNCIL AND THE INFALLIBILITY OF THE POPE—*continued* 53

BREACH WITH HISTORY, NO. 2. FROM THE HISTORY OF THE COUNCIL OF CONSTANCE. GALLICANISM.

V. THE VATICAN COUNCIL AND OBEDIENCE TO THE POPE 65

VI. REVIVED CLAIMS OF THE POPE 70

    1. TO THE DEPOSING POWER 70
    2. TO THE USE OF FORCE 75

CONTENTS.

		PAGE
VII. WARRANT OF ALLEGIANCE ACCORDING TO THE VATICAN		79
1. Its alleged Superiority		79
2. Its real Flaws		82
3. Alleged non-interference of the Popes for Two Hundred Years		88
VIII. ON THE INTRINSIC NATURE AND CONDITIONS OF THE PAPAL INFALLIBILITY DECREED IN THE VATICAN COUNCIL		92
IX. CONCLUSION		109
APPENDICES		121

VATICANISM.

I. INTRODUCTION.

THE number and quality of the antagonists, who have been drawn into the field on the occasion offered by my tract on the Vatican Decrees,* and the interest in the subject which has been manifested by the public of this and of many other countries, appear to show that it was not inopportune. The only special claim to attention with which I could invest it was this, that for thirty years I had striven hard, together with others, to secure a full measure of civil justice for my Roman Catholic fellow-countrymen, and that I still retained the convictions by which these efforts had been prompted. Knowing well the general indisposition of the English mind, amidst the pressing demands of our crowded daily life, to touch any subject comparatively abstract and remote, I was not surprised when many journals of great influence, reflecting this indisposition, condemned the publication of the Tract, and inspired Roman authorities among us with the vain conception that the discussion was not practical

---

* Appendix A.

or significant.* In Rome itself, a different view was taken; and the veiled prophets behind the throne, by whom the Latin Church is governed, brought about its condemnation as blasphemous, without perusal, from the lips of the Holy Father.† The object, probably, was at once to prevent or neutralise avowals of sympathy from Roman Catholic quarters. It may have been with a like aim that a number of Prelates at once entered, though by no means with one voice, into the lists. At length the great name of Dr. Newman was announced, and he too has replied to me, and explained himself, in a work to which I shall presently refer. Even apart from the *spolia opima* of this transcendent champion, I do not undervalue the ability, accomplishments, and discipline of that division of the Roman Army, which confronts our Church and nation. Besides its supply from indigenous sources, it has been strangely but very largely recruited from the ranks of the English Church, and her breasts have, for thirty years, been pierced mainly by the children whom they had fed.

In these replies, of which the large majority adopt without reserve the Ultramontane hypothesis, it is most commonly alleged that I have insulted the Roman Catholics of these kingdoms. Dr. Newman, averse to the use of harsh words, still announces (p. 3) that "heavy

---

* For example: "The various organs of the press, with the shrewd political sense for which they are conspicuous, without any possible collusion, extinguished its political import in a single morning."—Bishop Vaughan's 'Pastoral Letter,' p. 5.

† The declaration of *non avenu*, which, after a brief interval, followed the announcement of the condemnation, appeared upon some subsequent discussion to be negatived by the evidence. But such declarations are, I conceive, well understood in Rome to depend, like an English "*not at home*," upon convenience.

charges have been made against the Catholics of England." Bishop Clifford, in a pastoral letter of which I gladly acknowledge the equitable, restrained, and Christian spirit, says I have proclaimed that since the Vatican Decrees were published "it is no longer possible for English Catholics to pay to their temporal sovereign a full and undivided allegiance" (p. 5).

I am obliged to assert that not one of the writers against me has apprehended or stated with accuracy my principal charge. Except a prospective reference to "converts," the subject (to speak technically) of all my propositions is the word "Rome"; and with reference to these "converts," I speak of what they suffer, not of what they do. It is an entire, and even a gross, error to treat all affirmations about Rome as equivalent to affirmations about British subjects of the Roman communion. They may adopt the acts of Rome: the question was and is, whether they do. I have done nothing to leave this question open to doubt; for I have paraphrased my monosyllable "Rome" by the words "the Papal Chair, and its advisers and abettors" (p. 9). Unable as I am to attenuate the charges, on the contrary bound rather to plead guilty to the fault of having understated them, I am on that account the more anxious that their aim shall be clearly understood. First, then, I must again speak plainly, and I fear hardly, of that system, political rather than religious, which in Germany is well termed Vaticanism. It would be affectation to exclude from my language and meaning its contrivers and conscious promoters. But here in my mind, as well as in my page, anything approaching to censure stops. The Vatican Decrees do, in the strictest sense, establish for the Pope a supreme command over loyalty and civil duty. To the vast majority of Roman Catholics they are, and in all likelihood will long in their carefully enveloped meaning remain, practically unknown. Of that small minority, who have spoken or fitted themselves to speak, a portion reject them. Another portion receive them with an express reserve, to me perfectly satisfactory, against all their civil consequences. Another portion seem to suspend their judgment until it is determined what is a free Council, what is moral unanimity, what are declarations *ex cathedrâ*, whether there has been a decisive and binding promulgation so as to create a law, and whether the claim for an undue obedience need be considered until some act of undue obedience is asked. A very large class, as it seems to me, think they receive these Decrees, and do not. They are involved in inconsistency, and that inconsistency is dangerous. So I presume they would tell me that when I recite in the Creed the words, "I believe in the Holy Catholic Church," I am involved in inconsistency, and my inconsistency is dangerous. To treat this as a "heavy charge" is surely inaccurate; to call it an insult is (forgive the word) preposterous.

Not even against men who voted under pressure, against their better mind, for these deplorable Decrees, nay, not even against those who resisted them and now enforce them, is it for me to utter a word of censure. The just appreciation of their difficulties, the judgment of their conduct, lies in a region far too high for me. To assail the system is the Alpha and Omega of my desire; and it is to me matter of regret that I am not able to handle it as it deserves without reflecting upon the persons, be they who they may, that have brought it into the world; have sedulously fed it in its weakness; have reared it up to its baleful maturity; have forced it upon those, who now force it upon others; are obtaining for it from day to day fresh command over the pulpit, the press, the confessional, the teacher's chair, the bishop's throne; so that every father of a family, and every teacher in the Latin communion, shall, as he dies, be replaced by some one more deeply imbued with the new colour, until at the last, in that moiety of the whole Christian family, nothing shall remain except an Asian monarchy; nothing, but one giddy height of despotism, and one dead level of religious subserviency.

But even of the most responsible abettors of that system I desire once for all to say, that I do not presume in any way to impeach their sincerity; and that, as far as I am acquainted with their personal characters, I should think it great presumption to place myself in comparison or competition with any of them.

So much for insult. Much has also been said of my ignorance and incapacity in theology;[*] a province which I had entered only at the points where it crossed the border of the civil domain. Censures of this kind have great weight, when they follow upon demonstration given of errors committed by the person who is the object of them; but they can have very little, when they are used as substitutes for such a demonstration. In the absence of such proof, they can rank no higher than as a mere artifice of controversy. I have endeavoured to couch all my positive

---

[*] For example:—By Archbishop Manning, pp. 13, 177. Bishop Ullathorne, Letter, p. 10. 'Exposition Unravelled,' p. 68. Bishop Vaughan, p. 37. 'Month,' December, 1874, p. 497. Monk of St. Augustine's, p. 10. With these legitimate reproaches is oddly combined on the part of the Archbishop, and, apparently, of Bishop Ullathorne, a supposition that Dr. Döllinger was in some manner concerned in my tract on the Vatican Decrees. See Appendix B.

statements in language of moderation, and not one among them that appertains to the main line of argument has been shaken. As to the use of rhetoric, another matter of complaint, I certainly neither complain of strong language used against me, nor do I think that it can properly be avoided, when the matters of fact, carefully ascertained and stated, are such that it assists towards a comprehension of their character and consequences. At the same time, in the use of such language earnestness should not be allowed to degenerate into dogmatism, and to qualify is far more pleasant than to employ it.

With so much of preface, I proceed to execute my twofold duty. One of its branches is to state in what degree I conceive the immediate purpose of my Expostulation to have been served; and the other, to examine whether the allegations of antagonists have dislodged my arguments from their main positions, or, on the contrary, have confirmed them; and to re-state, nay, even to enlarge, those positions accordingly.

In considering the nature of the declarations on civil duty which have been elicited, it will not be thought unnatural if I begin with the words of one to whom age and fame combine in assigning the most conspicuous place —I mean Dr. Newman.

Of this most remarkable man I must pause to speak a word. In my opinion, his secession from the Church of England has never yet been estimated among us at anything like the full amount of its calamitous importance. It has been said that the world does not know its greatest men; neither, I will add, is it aware of the power and weight carried by the words and by the acts of those among its greatest men, whom it does know. The Ecclesiastical historian will perhaps hereafter judge that this secession was a much greater event even than the partial secession of John Wesley, the only case of personal loss suffered by the Church of England, since the Reformation, which can be at all compared with it in magnitude. I do not refer to its effect upon the mere balance of schools or parties in the Church; that is an inferior question. I refer to its effect upon the state of positive belief, and the attitude and capacities of the religious mind of England. Of this, thirty years ago, he had the leadership; an office and power from which none but himself could eject him.

> " Quis desiderio sit pudor aut modus
> Tam cari capitis?"

It has been his extraordinary, perhaps unexampled case, at a critical period, first to give to the religious thought of his time and country the most powerful impulse which for a long time it had received from any individual; and then to be the main though, without doubt, involuntary cause of disorganising it in a manner as remarkable, and breaking up its forces into a multitude of not only severed but conflicting bands.

My duty calls me to deal freely with his Letter to the Duke of Norfolk. But in doing so, I can never lose the recollection of the perhaps ill-appreciated greatness of his early life and works. I do not presume to intrude into the sanctuary of his present thoughts; but, by reason of that life and those works, it seems to me that there is something we must look upon with an affection, like that of Americans for those Englishmen who lived and wrought before the colonisation, or the severance, of their country. Nay, it may not be presumptuous to say we have a possessory right in the better half of him. All he produces is and must be most notable. But has he outrun, has he overtaken the greatness of the 'History of the Arians' and of the 'Parochial Sermons,' those indestructible classics of English theology?

And again, I thankfully record the admissions, which such integrity, combined with such acuteness, has not been able to withhold. They are of the greatest importance to the vindication of my argument. In my reading of his work, we have his authority for the following statements. That Roman Catholics are bound to be "as loyal as other subjects of the State;" and that Rome is not to give to the civil power " trouble or alarm " (p. 7). That the assurances given by the Roman Catholic Bishops in 1825-6 have not been strictly fulfilled (pp. 12-14). That Roman Catholics cannot wonder that statesmen should feel themselves aggrieved (p. 17). That Popes are sometimes in the wrong, and sometimes to be resisted, even in matters affecting the government and welfare of the Church (pp. 33, 34). That the Deposing power is defensible only upon condition of "the common consent of peoples" (p. 37). That if England supported Italy against any violent attempt to restore the Pope to his throne, Roman Catholics could offer no opposition but such as the constitution of the country allows (p. 49). That a soldier or sailor employed in a war which (in his private judgment, be it observed) he did not think unjust, ought not to retire from the prosecution of that war on the command of the Pope (p. 52). That conscience is the aboriginal vicar of Christ (p. 57): *ein tüchtiges Wort!* and Dr. Newman, at an ideal public dinner, will drink to conscience first, and the Pope afterwards (p. 66). That one of the great dangers of the Roman Catholic Church is to be found in the exaggerated language and proceedings allowed among its own members (pp. 4, 80, 94, 125), and that there is much *malaria* in the court of Rome. That a definition by a general Council, which the Pope approves, is not absolutely binding thereby, but requires a moral unanimity, and a subsequent reception by the Church (pp. 96-8). That antecedently to the theological definitions of 1854 and 1870, an opponent might have "fairly said" "it might appear that there were no sufficient historical grounds in behalf of either of them ;" and that the confutation of such an opponent is now to be sought only in "the fact of the definition being made" (p. 107). I shall indulge in none of the taunts, which Dr. Newman anticipates, on the want of correspondence between him and other Apologists; and I shall leave it to theologians to examine the bearing of these admissions on the scheme of Vaticanism, and on other parts of his own work. It is enough for me to record that, even if they stood alone, they would suffice to justify the publication which has given "occasion" for them; and that on the point of Dr. Newman's practical reservation of his command over his own "loyalty and civil duty," they are entirely satisfactory. As regards this latter point, the Pastoral of Bishop Clifford is also everything that can be wished. Among laymen who declare they accept the Decrees of 1870, I must specially make the same avowal as to my esteemed friend Mr. De Lisle ; and again, as to Mr. Stores Smith, who regards me with "silent and intense contempt," but who does not scruple to write as follows :—

"If this country decide to go to war, for any cause whatsoever, I will hold my own opinion as to the justice or policy of that war, but I will do all that in me lies to bring victory to the British standard. If there be any Parliamentary or Municipal election, and any Priest or Bishop, backed by Archbishop and the Pope, advise me to take a certain line of action, and I conceive that the opposite course is necessary for the general weal of my fellow-countrymen, I shall take the opposite."*

When it is considered that Dr. Newman is like the sun in the intellectual hemisphere of Anglo-Romanism, and that, besides those acceptors of the Decrees who write in the same sense, various Roman Catholics of weight and distinction, well known to represent the views of many more, have held equally outspoken and perhaps more consistent language, I cannot but say that the immediate purpose of my appeal has been attained, in so far that the loyalty of our Roman Catholic fellow-subjects in the mass remains evidently untainted and secure.

It would be unjust to Archbishop Manning, on whose opinions, in many points, I shall again have to animadvert, were I not to say that his declarations † also materially assist in leading me to this conclusion; an avowal I am the more bound to make, because I think the premisses from which he draws them are such as, if I were myself to accept them, would certainly much impair the guarantees for my performing, under all circumstances, the duties of a good subject.

This means that the poison, which circulates from Rome, has not actually been taken into the system. Unhappily, what I may term the minority among the Apologists do not represent the *ecclesia docens*; the silent diffusion of its influence in the lay atmosphere; the true current and aim of thought in the Papal Church, now given up to Vaticanism *de jure*, and likely, according to all human probability, to come from year to year more under its power. And here again the ulterior purpose of my Tract has been

---

* Letter in 'Halifax Courier' of December 5, 1874.
† Archbishop Manning, 'Vatican Decrees,' pp. 136–40.

thus far attained. It was this. To provide that if, together with the ancient and loyal traditions of the body, we have now imported among us a scheme adverse to the principles of human freedom and in its essence unfaithful to civil duty, the character of that scheme should be fully considered and understood. It is high time that the chasm should be made visible, severing it, and all who knowingly and thoroughly embrace it, from the principles which we had a right to believe not only prevailed among the Roman Catholics of these countries, but were allowed and recognised by the authorities of their Church; and would continue, therefore, to form the basis of their system, permanent and undisturbed. For the more complete attainment of this object, I must now proceed to gather together the many threads of the controversy, as it has been left by my numerous opponents. This I shall do, not from any mere call of speculation or logical consistency, but for strong practical reasons.

Dr. Newman's letter to the Duke of Norfolk is of the highest interest as a psychological study. Whatever he writes, whether we agree with him or not, presents to us this great attraction as well as advantage, that we have everywhere the man in the work, that his words are the transparent covering of his nature. If there be obliquity in them, it is purely intellectual obliquity; the work of an intellect sharp enough to cut the diamond, and bright as the diamond which it cuts. How rarely it is found, in the wayward and inscrutable records of our race, that with these instruments of an almost superhuman force and subtlety, robustness of character and energy of will are or can be developed in the same extraordinary proportions, so as to integrate that structure of combined thought and action, which makes life a moral whole! "There are gifts too large and too fearful to be handled freely."* But I turn from an incidental reflection to observe that my duty is to appreciate the letter of Dr. Newman exclusively in relation to my Tract. I thankfully here record, in the first place, the kindliness of his tone. If he has striven to minimise the Decrees of the Vatican, I am certain he has also striven to minimise his censures, and has put words aside before they touched his paper, which must have been in his thoughts, if not upon his pen. I sum up this pleasant portion of my duty with the language of Helen respecting Hector: πατὴρ ὣς ἤπιος αἰεί.†

It is, in my opinion, an entire mistake to suppose that theories like those, of which Rome is the centre, are not operative on the thoughts and actions of men. An army of teachers, the largest and the most compact in the world, is ever sedulously at work to bring them into practice. Within our own time they have most powerfully, as well as most injuriously, altered the spirit and feeling of the Roman Church at large; and it will be strange indeed if, having done so much in the last half-century, they shall effect nothing in the next. I must avow, then, that I do not feel exactly the same security for the future as for the present. Still less do I feel the same security for other lands as for this. Nor can I overlook indications which lead to the belief that, even in this country, and at this time, the proceedings of Vaticanism threaten to be a source of some practical inconvenience. I am confident that if a system so radically bad is to be made or kept innocuous, the first condition for attaining such a result is that its movements should be carefully watched,

---

* Dr. Newman, p. 127.   † Iliad, xxiv. 770.

and, above all, that the bases on which they work should be faithfully and unflinchingly exposed. Nor can I quit this portion of the subject without these remarks. The satisfactory views of Archbishop Manning on the present rule of civil allegiance have not prevented him from giving his countenance as a responsible editor* to the lucubrations of a gentleman, who denies liberty of conscience, and asserts the right to persecute when there is the power; a right which, indeed, the Prelate has not himself disclaimed.

Nor must it be forgotten, that the very best of all the declarations we have heard from those who allow themselves to be entangled in the meshes of the Vatican Decrees, are, every one of them, uttered subject to the condition that, upon orders from Rome, if such orders should issue, they shall be qualified, or retracted, or reversed.

"A breath can *un*make them, as a breath has made."

But even apart from all this, do what we may in checking external developments, it is not in our power to neutralise the mischiefs of the wanton aggression of 1870 upon the liberties—too scanty, it is excusable to think —which up to that epoch had been allowed to private Christians in the Roman communion. Even in those parts of Christendom where the Decrees and the present attitude of the Papal See do not produce or aggravate open broils with the civil power, by undermining moral liberty they impair moral responsibility, and silently, in the succession of generations if not even in the lifetime of individuals, tend to emasculate the vigour of the mind.

In the tract on the Vatican Decrees I passed briefly by those portions of my original statement which most

---

* 'Essays,' edited by Archbishop Manning, pp. 401-5, 467.

lay within the province of theology, and dwelt principally on two main propositions.

I. That Rome had reproduced for active service those doctrines of former times, termed by me "rusty tools," which she was fondly thought to have disused.

II. That the Pope now claims, with plenary authority, from every convert and member of his Church, that he "shall place his loyalty and civil duty at the mercy of another :" that other being himself.

These are the assertions, which I now hold myself bound further to sustain and prove.

II. THE RUSTY TOOLS. THE SYLLABUS.

1. *Its Contents.*
2. *Its Authority.*

WITH regard to the proposition that Rome has refurbished her "rusty" tools, Dr. Newman says it was by these tools that Europe was brought into a civilized condition: and thinks it worth while to ask whether it is my wish that penalties so sharp, and expressions so high, should be of daily use.*

I may be allowed to say, in reply to the remark I have cited, that I have nowhere presumed to pronounce a general censure on the conduct of the Papacy in the middle ages. That is a vast question, reaching far beyond my knowledge or capacity. I believe much is to be justly said in praise, much as justly in blame. But I cannot view the statement that Papal claims and conduct created the civilization of Europe as other than thoroughly unhistorical and one-sided: as resting upon a narrow selection of evidence, upon strong exaggeration of what that evidence imports, and upon an "invincible ignorance" as to all the rest.

Many things may have been suited, or not unsuited, to rude times and indeterminate ideas of political right, the reproduction of which is at the least strange, perhaps even monstrous. We look back with interest and respect upon our early fire-arms as they rest peacefully ranged upon

---

* Dr. Newman, p. 32.

the wall; but we cannot think highly of the judgment which would recommend their use in modern warfare. As for those weapons which had been consigned to obscurity and rust, my answer to Dr. Newman's question is that they should have slept for ever, till perchance some reclaiming plough of the future should disturb them.

" . . . quum finibus illis
Agricola, incurvo terram molitus aratro,
Exesa inveniet scabrâ rubigine pila."*

As to the proof of my accusation, it appeared to me that it might be sufficiently given in a summary but true account† of some important portions of the Encyclica of December 8th, 1864, and especially of the accompanying Syllabus of the same date.

The replies to the five or six pages, in which I dealt with this subject, have so swollen as to reach fifteen or twenty times the bulk. I am sorry that they involve me in the necessity of entering upon a few pages of detail which may be wearisome. But I am bound to vindicate my good faith and care, where a failure in either involves results of real importance. These results fall under the two following heads:—

(1). The Syllabus; what is its language?
(2). The Syllabus; what is its authority?

As to the language, I have justly represented it: as to its authority, my statement is not above, but below the mark.

---

* Virgil, Georgics i. 493.

† Erroneously called by some of my antagonists a translation, and then condemned as a bad translation. But I know of no *recipe* for translating into less than half the bulk of the original.

1. *The Contents of the Syllabus.*

My representation of the language of the Syllabus has been assailed in strong terms. I proceed to defend it: observing, however, that my legitimate object was to state in popular terms the effect of propositions more or less technical and scholastic: and, secondly, that I did not present each and every proposition for a separate disapproval, but directed attention rather to the effect of the document as a whole, in a qualifying passage (p. 13) which no one of my critics has been at the pains to notice.

Nos. 1–3.—The first charge of unjust representation is this.* I have stated that the Pope condemns (p. 25) liberty of the press, and liberty of speech. By reference to the original it is shown, that the right of printing and speaking is not in terms condemned universally; but only the right of each man to print or speak all his thoughts (*suos conceptus quoscunque*), whatever they may be. Hereupon it is justly observed, that in all countries there are laws against blasphemy, or obscenity, or sedition, or all three. It is argued, then, that men are not allowed the right to speak or print *all* their thoughts, and that such an extreme right only is what the Pope has condemned.

It appears to me that this is, to use a mild phrase, mere trifling with the subject. We are asked to believe that what the Pope intended to condemn was a state of things, which never has existed in any country of the world. Now, he says he is condemning one of the commonly prevailing errors of the time, familiarly known

---

* 'The Month,' December 1874. p. 494. !Coleridge, ' Abomination of Desolation,' p. 20. Bishop Ullathorne, ' Pastoral Letter,' p. 16. Monk of St. Augustine's, p. 15. Dr. Newman, pp. 59, 72, in some part.

to the bishops whom he addresses.* What bishop knows of a State which by law allows a perfectly free course to blasphemy, filthiness, and sedition? The world knows quite well what is meant by free speech and a free press. It does mean, generally, perhaps it may be said universally, the right of declaring all opinions whatsoever. The limit of freedom is not the justness of the opinion, but it is this, that it shall be opinion in good faith, and not mere grossness, passion, or appeal to violence. The law of England at this moment, allowing all opinions whatever, provided they are treated by way of rational discourse, most closely corresponds to what the Pope has condemned. His condemnation is illustrated by his own practice as Governor in the Roman States, where no opinion could be spoken or printed but such as he approved. Once, indeed, he permitted a free discussion on Saint Peter's presence and prelacy in the city; but he repented quickly, and forbade the repetition of it. We might even cite his practice as Pope in 1870, where everything was done to keep the proceedings of the Council secret from the Church which it professed to represent, and even practically secret from its members, except those who were of the governing cabal. But there can be no better mode of exhibiting his real meaning than by referring to his account of the Austrian law. *Hâc lege omnis omnium opinionum et librariæ artis libertas, omnis tum fidei, tum conscientiæ ac doctrinæ, libertas statuitur.*† To the kind of condemnation given, I shall again

---

* "Probè noscitis hoc tempore non paucos reperiri, qui," &c.—'Encycl.,' December 8, 1864.

† From the Pope's Allocution of June 22, 1868: "By this law is established universal liberty of all opinions and of the press, and, as of belief, so of conscience and of teaching." See Vering,

refer; but the matter of it is nothing abstract or imaginary, it is actual freedom of thinking, speaking, and printing, as it is practised in a great civilized and Christian empire. I repel, then, the charge against me as no better than a verbal subterfuge; and I again affirm that in his Syllabus, as in his acts, the Pope has condemned liberty of speech and liberty of the press.

No. 5.—I have stated that the Pope condemns " those who assign to the State the power of defining the civil rights (*jura*) and province of the Church." Hereupon it is boldly stated that " the word civil is a pure interpolation."* This statement Dr. Newman's undertaking tempts him to quote, but his sagacity and scholarship save him from adopting. Anticipating some cavil such as this, I took care (which is not noticed) to place the word *jura* in my text. I now affirm that my translation is correct. *Jus* means, not right at large, but a specific form of right, and in this case civil right, to which meaning indeed the word constantly leans. It refers to right which is social, relative, extrinsic. *Jus hominum situm est in generis humani societate* (Cic. Tusc. ii. 26). If a theological definition is desired, take that of Dens: *Accipitur potissimum pro jure prout est in altero, cui debet satisfieri ad æqualitatem; de jure sic sumpto hic agitur.*† It is not of the internal constitution of the Church and the rights of its members *inter se* that the proposition treats; nor yet of its ecclesiastical standing in reference to other bodies; but of its rights in the face of the State; that is to say, of

---

Archiv für Katholisches Kirchenrecht.' Mainz, 1868, p. 171, Band xx.
* 'The Abomination of Desolation,' p. 21. Dr. Newman, p. 87.
† 'Tractatus de jure et justitiâ,' No. 6.

its civil rights. My account therefore was accurate; and Mr. Coleridge's criticism superfluous.

I must, however, admit that Vaticanism has a way of escape. For perhaps it does not admit that the Church enjoys any civil rights: but considers as her own, and therefore spiritual in their source, such rights as we consider accidental and derivative, even where not abusive.

On this subject I will refer to a high authority. The Jesuit Schrader was, I believe, one of those employed in drawing up the Syllabus. He has published a work, with a Papal Approbation attached to it, in which he converts the condemnatory negations of the Syllabus into the corresponding affirmatives. For Article XXX. he gives the following proposition :—

"The immunities of the Church, and of ecclesiastical persons, have not their origin in civil right."

He adds the remark: "but are rooted in the Church's own right, given to her from God." *

No. 7.—I have said those persons are condemned by the Syllabus, who hold that in countries called Catholic the free exercise of other religions may laudably be allowed. Dr. Newman truly observes,† that it is the free exercise of religion by immigrants or foreigners which is meant (hominibus *illuc immigrantibus*), and that I have omitted the words. I omitted them, for my case was strong enough without them. But they seem to strengthen my case. For the claim to a free exercise of religion on behalf of immigrants or foreigners is a stronger one than on behalf of natives, and has been so recognised in Italy and in

---

* 'Der Papst und die Modernen Ideen.' Von P. Clemens Schrader, S.J. Heft ii. 65.

† Dr. Newman, p. 86.

Rome itself. I think I am right in saying that difference of tongue has generally been recognised by Church law as mitigating the objections to the toleration of dissidence. And it is this stronger claim, not the weaker one, which is condemned. So that if there be a fault, it is the fault of under-, not of over-statement.

Again I support myself by the high authority of Schrader the Jesuit. The following is his Article LXXVII. It draws no distinction of countries:—

"In our view it is still useful that the Catholic religion should be maintained as the only State religion to the exclusion of every other."*

In the appended remark he observes, that *on this account* the Pope, in 1856, condemned the then recent Spanish law which tolerated other forms of worship.†

No. 8.—I am charged, again,‡ with mistranslating under my eighth head. The condemnation in the Syllabus is, as I conceived, capable of being construed to apply to the entire proposition as it is there given, or to a part of it only. In brief it is this: "The Episcopate has a certain power not inherent, but conferred by the State, which may therefore be withdrawn at the pleasure of the State." The condemnation might be aimed at the assertion that such a power exists, or at the assertion that it is withdrawable at pleasure. In the latter sense, the condemnation is unwise and questionable as a general proposition: in the former sense it is outrageous beyond all bounds; and I am boldly accused of mistranslating‡ because I chose the milder imputation of the two, and understood the censure to apply only to withdrawal *ad libitum*. I learn now that, in the

---

* Schrader, p. 80.
† *Infra.*
‡ Mr. Coleridge, 'Abomination of Desolation,' p. 21.

opinion of this antagonist at least, the State was not the source of (for example) the power of coinage, which was at one time exercised by the Bishops of Durham. So that the upshot is: either my construction is right, or my charge is milder than it should have been.

Nos. 13, 14.—A grave charge is made against me respecting the matrimonial propositions: because I have cited the Pope as condemning those who affirm that the matrimonial contract is binding whether there is or is not (according to the Roman doctrine) a Sacrament; and have not at the same time stated that English marriages are held by Rome to be Sacramental, and therefore valid.*

No charge, serious or slight, could be more entirely futile. But it is serious and not slight; and those who prompt the examination must abide the recoil. I begin thus:—

1. I am censured for not having given ⌈distinctions between one country and another, which the Pope himself has not given.

2. And which are also thought unnecessary by authorised expounders of the Syllabus for the faithful.†

I have before me the Exposition,‡ with the text, of the Encyclica and Syllabus, published at Cologne in 1874, with the approval of authority (*mit oberkirchlicher Approbation*). In p. 45 it is distinctly taught that with marriage the State has nothing to do; that it may safely rely upon the Church; that civil marriage, in the eyes of the Church, is only concubinage; and that the State, by the use of worldly compulsion, prevents the two concubinary

---

* Monk of St. Augustine's, p. 15. 'Abomination,' p. 22.
† Appendix B.
‡ '*Die Encyclica, der Syllabus, und die wichtigsten darin angeführten Actenstücke, nebst einer ausführlichen Einleitung.*' Köln, 1874.

parties from repenting and abandoning their guilty relation to one another. Exactly the same is the doctrine of the Pope himself, in his Speeches published at Rome; where civil marriage is declared to be, for Christians, nothing more than a mere concubinage, and a filthy concubinage (*sozzo concubinato*).* These extraordinary declarations are not due to the fondness of the Pontiff for speaking *impromptu*. In his letter of September 19th, 1852, to King Victor Emmanuel, he declares that matrimony carrying the sacrament is alone lawful for Christians, and that a law of civil marriage, which goes to divide them for practical purposes, constitutes a concubinage in the guise of legitimate marriage.† So that, in truth, in all countries within the scope of these denunciations, the parties to a civil marriage are declared to be living in an illicit connection, which they are called upon to renounce. This call is addressed to them separately as well as jointly, the wife being summoned to leave her husband, and the husband to abandon his wife; and after this pretended repentance from a state of sin, unless the law of the land and fear of consequences prevail, a new connection, under the name of a marriage, may be formed with the sanction of the Church of Rome. It is not possible, in the limited space here at my command, adequately to exhibit a state of facts, thus created by the highest authorities of the Roman Church, which I shall now not shrink from calling horrible and revolting in itself, and dangerous to the morals of society, the structure of the family, and the peace of life.

---

* 'Discorsi di Pio IX.' Roma, 1872, 1873. Vol. i. p. 193, vol. ii. p. 355.

† 'Recueil des Allocutions de Pie IX.' &c. Paris: Leclerc, 1865, p. 312.

It is true, indeed, that the two hundred thousand non-Roman marriages, which are annually celebrated in England, do not at present fall under the foul epithets of Rome. But why? Not because we marry, as I believe nineteen-twentieths of us marry, under the sanctions of religion; for our marriages are, in the eye of the Pope, purely civil marriages; but only for the technical, accidental, and precarious reason, that the disciplinary decrees of Trent are not canonically in force in this country. There is nothing, unless it be motives of mere policy, to prevent the Pope from giving them force here when he pleases. If, and when that is done, every marriage thereafter concluded in the English Church will, according to his own words, be a filthy concubinage.

The decrees have force already in many parts of Germany, and in many entire countries of Europe. Within these limits, every civil marriage, and every religious marriage not contracted before a Roman *parochus*, as the Council of Trent requires, is but the formation of a guilty connection, which each of the parties severally is charged by the Church of Rome to dissolve, under pain of being held to be in mortal sin.

In 1602, when the Decree of Trent had been in force for thirty-eight years, it was applied by the *Congregatio Concilii*, with the approval of Pope Clement VIII., to non-Roman marriages, by a declaration that heretics were bound to conform (which was impossible) to the rules of the Council, in default of which their marriages, whether religious or civil, were null and void.*

---

* "Hæreticos quoque, ubi Decretum dicti capitis est publicatum, teneri talem formam observare, et propterea ipsorum etiam matrimonia, absque formâ Concilii quamvis coram ministro hæretico vel magistratu loci contracta, nulla atque irrita esse."—Vering, Archiv, xvii. 461, *seq. See* Sicherer, 'Eherecht in Bayern,' Munich, 1875, p. 12, n.

To this portentous rule exceptions have been made, especially by Benedict XIV. in the case of Holland. Indeed, he questioned its propriety; and Pius VII., in a communication to the Primate Dalberg, formerly Archbishop of Mentz, referred with approval to the language of Benedict XIV. Many theologians have held an opinion adverse to it, and clergy have been allowed to act at times upon that opinion, but only under cover of a policy of dissimulation, a name by which the Court of Rome itself has not been ashamed to describe its own conduct.* But when the abrogation of the rule for non-Roman marriages has been prayed for, even by Bishops, and bodies of Bishops, the prayer has failed.† It has been kept alive; and transactions positively dreadful have taken place under its authority, and under other provisions calculated for the same end. Perrone, who may be called the favourite theologian of the Curia, points out that it works for the benefit of heretics, as on their conversion it has often given them an opportunity of contracting a new marriage; during the lifetime, that is to say, of the former wife.‡

The upshot, then, seems to be this: that Rome, while stigmatising marriages not Tridentine as concubinages in the manner we have seen, reserves a power, under the name or plea of special circumstances, to acknowledge them or not, as policy may recommend. This is but

---

* Sicherer, ibid., p. 37, n. 56, 58.
† Sicherer, ibid., p. 66, n.
‡ "Si quid ex hâc doctrinâ et praxi provenit, vertitur demum in bonum ipsorum acatholicorum, si quando contingat eos in Ecclesiæ Catholicæ sinum redire, dum ipsis indulgetur, ita poscentibus rerum adjunctis, vel ob mutua dissidia, vel ob separationem ab invicem, aliaque ejusmodi, novas inire nuptias, uti ex non paucis resolutionibus liquet: aut proprium instaurare conjugium, si ambo convertantur conjuges." 'De Matrim. Christ.,' ii. 245, ed. Rome, 1856.

the old story. All problems, which menace the Roman Chair with difficulties it dare not face, are to be solved, not by the laying down of principles, good or bad, strict or lax, in an intelligible manner, but by reserving all cases as matters of discretion to the breast of the *Curia*, which will decide from time to time, according to its pleasure, whether there has been a sacrament or not, and whether we are married folks, or persons living in guilty commerce, and rearing our children under a false pretext of legitimacy.

This, then, is the statement I now make. It has been drawn from me by the exuberant zeal and precipitate accusations of the school of Loyola.

No. 18.—Finally, it is contended that I misrepresent Rome in stating that it condemns the call to reconcile itself with progress, liberalism, and modern civilization.

It is boldly stated that the Pope condemns not these, but only what is bad in these.* And thus it is that, to avert public displeasure, words are put into the Pope's mouth, which he has not used, and which are at variance with the whole spirit of the document that he has sent forth to alarm, as Dr. Newman too well sees, the educated mind of Europe.† It appears to be claimed for Popes, that they shall be supreme over the laws of language. But mankind protests against a system which palters in a double sense with its own solemn declarations; imposing them on the weak, glorying in them before those who are favourably prepossessed, and then contracting their sense *ad libitum*, even to the point of nullity, by arbitrary interpolation, to appease the scandalised understanding of

---

* 'The Month,' as *sup*. p. 496.   Bishop Ullathorne, 'Expostulation Unravelled,' p. 69.

† Dr. Newman, p. 90.

Christian nations. Without doubt progress, liberalism, modern civilization, are terms more or less ambiguous; but they are, under a sound general rule, determinable by the context. Now, the contexts of the Syllabus and Encyclica are perfectly unambiguous; they perfectly explain what the Pope means by the words. He means to condemn all that we consider fair limitation of the claims of priestly power; to repudiate the title of man to general freedom of thought, and of speech in all its varied forms of utterance; the title of a nation to resist those, who treat the sovereignty over it as a property, and who would enforce on the people—for example, of the Papal States—a government independently of or against its will; in a word, the true and only sure titles of freedom in all its branches, inward and outward, mental, moral and political, as they are ordinarily understood in the judgment of this age and country.

I have gone, I believe, through every particular impeachment of my account of the language of the Syllabus and the Encyclica. If each and all of these have failed, I presume that I need not dwell upon the general allegations of opponents in respect to those heads where they have not been pleased to enter upon details.*

Now, it is quite idle to escape the force of these charges by reproaches aimed at my unacquaintance with theology, and by recommendations, sarcastic or sincere, that I should obtain some instruction in its elements. To such reproaches I shall peacefully and respectfully bow, so soon as I shall have been convicted of error. But I think I have shown that the only variations from exact truth, to which I can

---

* 'The Month,' as *sup.* p. 497.

plead guilty, are variations in the way of understatements of the case which it was my duty to produce.

2. *The Authority of the Syllabus.*

I have next to inquire what is the authority of the Syllabus?

Had I been inclined to push my case to extremes, I might very well have contended that this document was delivered *ex cathedrâ*. Schulte, whose authority as a Canonist is allowed on all hands to be great, founds his argument on that opinion.* Dr. Ward, who has been thanked† by His Holiness for his defence of the faith, wonders that any one can doubt it.‡ The Pope himself, in his speeches, couples the Syllabus with the Decrees of the Vatican Council, as being jointly the great fundamental teachings of these latter days; and he even describes it as the only anchor of safety for the coming time.§ Bishop Fessler, whose work was published some time after the Council, to tone down alarms, and has had a formal approval from the Pope,‖ holds that the Syllabus is not a document proceeding *ex cathedrâ*. But it touches faith and morals: its condemnations are, and are allowed to be, assertions of their contradictories, into which assertions they have been formally converted by Schrader, a writer of authority, who was officially employed in its compilation. Furthermore, though I was wrong (as Dr. Newman has properly observed¶) in assuming that the Encyclica directly covered all the propositions of the Syllabus, yet

---

* 'Power of the Roman Popes' (Transl. by Sommers. Adelaide, 1871).
† 'Dublin Review,' July, 1870, p. 224.
‡ *Ibid.* July, 1874, p. 9.
§ 'Discorsi di Pio IX.,' vol. i. p. 59.
‖ Fessler, 'True and False Infallibility,' English transl., p. iii.
¶ Newman, p. 82.

this document is addressed by the Pope through Cardinal Antonelli to all the Bishops of the Christian (Papal) world, therefore in his capacity as universal Teacher.

The reasons advanced by Bishop Fessler in the opposite sense appear to be very weak. When the Pope (by conversion of the 23rd Proposition) declares that preceding pontiffs have not exceeded the limits of their power, and have not usurped the rights of princes, Bishop Fessler replies that we are here dealing only with facts of history, not touching faith or morals, so that there is no subject-matter for a dogmatic definition.* But the depositions of sovereigns were often founded on such considerations; as when Gregory VII., in A.D. 1079, charged upon Henry IV. many capital crimes,† and as when Innocent III. deposed Raymond of Toulouse for (among other reasons) not proceeding satisfactorily with the extirpation of the Albigenses.‡ The Christian creed itself is chiefly composed of matters of fact set forth as articles of belief. And apart from this, he who asserts, that the acts of Popes did not go beyond their rights, thereby avers his belief in the claims of right which those acts of deposition involved.

Fessler's other objection is, that the form of the Syllabus does not set forth the intention of the Pope.§ But he appears to have overlooked the perfectly explicit covering letter of Antonelli, which in the Pope's name transmits the Syllabus, in order that the whole body of Latin Bishops might have before their eyes those errors and false doctrines of the age which the Pope had proscribed. Nor does Fessler venture to assert, that the Syllabus is without

---

* Fessler, 'Vraie et fausse Infaillibilité des Papes,' French transl., p. 89.
† Greenwood, 'Cathedra Petri,' iv. 420.
‡ *Ibid.* v. 546.   § Fessler, p. 132.

dogmatic authority. He only says many theologians have doubts upon the question whether it be *ex cathedrâ*: theological science will hereafter have to examine and decide the matter :* in the meantime every Roman Catholic is bound to submit to and obey it. Such is the low or moderate doctrine concerning the Syllabus.† Thus its dogmatic authority is probable : its title to universal obedience is absolute, while among its assertions is that the Church has the right to employ force, and that the Popes have not exceeded their powers or invaded the rights of princes.

Now, when I turn to the seductive pages of Dr. Newman, I find myself to be breathing another air, and discussing, it would seem, some other Syllabus. If the Pope were the author of it, he would accept it.‡ But he is not,§ and no one knows who is. Therefore it has no dogmatic force.∥ It is an index to a set of dogmatic Bulls and Allocutions, but it is no more dogmatic itself than any other index, or table of contents.¶ Its value lies in its references, and from them alone can we learn its meaning.

If we had Dr. Newman for Pope, we should be tolerably safe, so merciful and genial would be his rule. But when Dr. Newman, not being Pope, contradicts and nullifies what the Pope declares, whatever we may wish, we cannot renounce the use of our eyes. Fessler, who writes, as Dr. Newman truly says, to curb exaggerations,** and who is approved by the Pope, declares†† that every subject of the Pope, and thus that Dr. Newman, is bound to obey the Syllabus, because it is from the Pope and of the Pope. "Before the Council of the Vatican, every Catholic was

---

* Fessler, pp. 8, 132, 134. † *Ibid.* p. 8.
‡ Newman, p. 20. § *Ibid.* p. 79.
∥ *Ibid.* p. 81. ¶ *Ibid.* p. 8.
** *Ibid.* p. 81. †† Fessler, p. 8 (Fr. trans.).

bound to submit to and obey the Syllabus: the Council of the Vatican has made no difference in that obligation of conscience." He questions its title, indeed, to be held as *ex cathedrâ*, and this is his main contention against Schulte; but he nowhere denies its infallibility, and he distinctly includes it in the range of Christian obedience.

Next, Dr. Newman lays it down that the words of the Syllabus are of no force in themselves, except as far as they correspond with the terms of the briefs to which references are given, and which he admits to be binding. But here Dr. Newman is in flat contradiction to the official letter of Cardinal Antonelli, who states that the Syllabus has been framed, and is sent to the Bishops, by command of the Pope, inasmuch as it is likely that they have by no means all seen the prior instruments, and in order that they may know from the Syllabus itself what it is that has been condemned. Thus then it will be seen that the Syllabus has been authoritatively substituted for the original documents as a guide to the Bishops. And if, as Dr. Newman says, and as I think in some cases is the fact, the propositions of the Syllabus widen the propositions of those documents, it is the wider and not the narrower form that binds, unless Dr. Newman is more in the confidence of Rome than the Secretary of the Vatican Council, and than the regular minister of the Pope.

Again, I am reminded by the 'Dublin Review,' a favoured organ of Roman opinions, that utterances *ex cathedrâ** are not the only form in which Infallibility can speak: and that the Syllabus, whether *ex cathedrâ* or not, since it has been uttered by the Pope, and accepted by the Church diffused, that is to say, by the Bishops diffused, is undoubtedly infallible. This would seem to be the

---
* 'Dublin Review,' Jan. 1875, pp. 177, 310.

opinion of Bishop Ullathorne.* But what is conclusive as to practical effect upon the whole case is this—that while not one among the Roman apologists admits that the Syllabus is or may be erroneous, the obligation to obey it is asserted on all hands, and is founded on the language of an infallible Vatican Decree.

I have been content to argue the case of the Syllabus upon the supposition that, in relation to this country at least, its declarations were purely abstract. The readers, however, of ' Macmillan's Magazine ' for February may perceive that even now we are not without a sample of its fruits in a matrimonial case, of which particulars were long ago given in the 'Times' newspaper, and which may possibly again become the object of public notice.

It is therefore absolutely superfluous to follow Dr. Newman through his references to the Briefs and Allocutions marginally noted. The Syllabus is part of that series of acts to which the dogmatisations of 1854 and 1870 also belong; and it bridges over the interval between them. It generalises, and advisedly enlarges, a number of particular condemnations; and, addressing them to all the Bishops, brings the whole of the Latin obedience within its net. The fish, when it is inclosed and beached, may struggle for a while : but it dies, while the fisherman lives, carries it to market, and quietly puts the price into his till.

The result then is :

1. I abide by my account of the contents of the Syllabus.

2. I have understated, not overstated, its authority.

3. It may be *ex cathedrâ*; it seems to have the infallibility of dogma : it unquestionably demands, and is entitled (in the code of Vaticanism) to demand, obedience.

---

* Bishop Ullathorne, ' Expost. Unravelled,' p. 66.

III. THE VATICAN COUNCIL AND THE INFALLIBILITY OF THE POPE.

Breach with History, No. 1.

LIKE the chieftains of the heroic time, Archbishop Manning takes his place with promptitude, and operates in front of the force he leads.

Upon the first appearance of my tract, he instantly gave utterance to the following propositions; nor has he since receded from them :

1. That the Infallibility of the Pope was a doctrine of Divine Faith before the Council of the Vatican was held.

2. That the Vatican Decrees have in no jot or tittle changed either the obligations or the conditions of civil allegiance.

3. That the civil allegiance of Roman Catholics is as undivided as that of other Christians, and neither more nor less limited.

4. That the claim of the Roman Church against obedience to the civil power in certain cases is the same as that made by other religious communions in this country.

These four propositions may be treated as two. The first is so allied with the second, and the third with the fourth, that the two members of each pair respectively must stand or fall together. I can make no objection to the manner in which they raise the question. I shall leave it to others, whom it may more concern, to treat that portion of his work in which, passing by matters that more nearly touched his argument, he has entered at large on the controversy between Rome and the German Empire; nor shall I now discuss his compendium of Italian history, which in no manner touches the question whether the dominion of the Pope ought again to be imposed by foreign arms upon a portion of the Italian people. But of the four propositions I will say that I accept them all, subject to the very simple condition that the word "not" be inserted in the three which are affirmative, and its equivalent struck out from the one which is negative.

Or, to state the case in my own words:

My task will be to make good the two following assertions, which were the principal subjects of my former argument:

1. That upon the authority, for many generations, of those who preceded Archbishop Manning and his coadjutors in their present official position, as well as upon other authority, Papal Infallibility was not "a doctrine of Divine Faith before the Council of the Vatican was held."

And that therefore the Vatican Decrees have changed the obligations and conditions of civil allegiance.

2. That the claim of the Papal Church against obedience to the civil power in certain cases not only goes beyond, but is essentially different from, that made by other religious communions or by their members in this country.

And that, therefore, the civil allegiance of those, who admit the claim, and carry it to its logical consequences, is not for the purposes of the State the same with that of other Christians, but is differently limited.

In his able and lengthened work, Archbishop Manning has found space for a dissertation on the great German quarrel, but has not included, in his proof of the belief in Papal Infallibility before 1870, any reference to the history of the Church over which he presides, or the sister Church in Ireland. This very grave deficiency I shall endeavour to make good, by enlarging and completing the statement briefly given in my tract. That statement was that the English and Irish penal laws against Roman Catholics were repealed on the faith of assurances, which have not been fulfilled.

Had all antagonists been content to reply with the simple ingenuousness of Dr. Newman, it might have been unnecessary to resume this portion of the subject. I make no complaint of the Archbishop; for such a reply would have destroyed his case. Dr. Newman, struggling hard with the difficulties of his task, finds that the statement of Dr. Doyle requires (p. 12) " some pious interpretation :" that in 1826 the clergy both of England and Ireland were trained in Gallican opinions (p. 13), and had modes of thinking " foreign altogether to the minds of the *entourage* of the Holy See :" that the British ministers ought to have applied to Rome (p. 14), to learn the civil duties of British subjects: and that " no pledge from Catholics was of any value, to which Rome was not a party."

This declaration involves all, and more than all, that I had ventured reluctantly to impute. Statesmen of the future, recollect the words, and recollect from whom they came: from the man who by his genius, piety, and learning, towers above all the eminences of the Anglo-papal communion; who, so declares a Romish organ,* " has been the mind and tongue to shape and express the English Catholic position in the many controversies which have arisen " since 1845, and who has been roused from his repose on this occasion only by the most fervid appeals to him as the man that could best teach his co-religionists how and what to think. The lesson received is this. Although pledges were given, although their validity

---

* 'The Month,' December, 1874, p. 461.

was firmly and even passionately* asserted, although the subject-matter was one of civil allegiance, "no pledge from Catholics was of any value, to which Rome was not a party" (p. 14).

In all seriousness I ask whether there is not involved in these words of Dr. Newman an ominous approximation to my allegation, that the seceder to the Roman Church "places his loyalty and civil duty at the mercy of another"?

But as Archbishop Manning has asserted that the Decrees of the Vatican have "in no jot or tittle" altered civil allegiance,† and that "before the Council was held, the infallibility of the Pope was a doctrine of Divine Faith,"‡ and as he is the official head of the Anglo-Roman body, I must test his assertions by one of those appeals to history, which he has sometimes said are treason to the Church: § as indeed they are, in his sense of the Church, and in his sense of treason. It is only justice to the Archbishop to add, that he does not stand alone. Bishop Ullathorne says, "The Pope always wielded this infallibility, and all men knew this to be the fact." ‖ We shall presently find some men, whose history the Bishop should have been familiar with, and who did not know this to be the fact, but very solemnly assured us they knew the exact contrary.

This is not an affair, as Dr. Newman seems to think, of a particular generation of clergy who had been edu-

---

* Bishop Doyle, 'Essay on the Claims,' p. 38.
† Letter to the 'Times,' Nov. 7, 1874.
‡ Letter to 'New York Herald,' Nov. 10, 1874. Letter to 'Macmillan's Magazine,' Oct. 22.
§ 'Temporal Mission of the Holy Ghost,' p. 226. 'The Vatican Council and its Definitions,' 1870, p. 119.
‖ Bishop Ullathorne, Letter, p. 14.

cated in Gallican opinions. In all times, from the reign of Elizabeth to that of Victoria, the lay Roman Catholics of England, as a body, have been eminently and unreservedly loyal. But they have been as eminently noted for their thorough estrangement from Ultramontane opinions; and their clergy, down to the period of the Emancipation Act, felt with them; though a school addicted to curialism and Jesuitism, thrust among them by the Popes at the commencement of the period, first brought upon them grievous sufferings, then succeeded in attaching a stigma to their name, and now threatens gradually to accomplish a transformation of their opinions, with an eventual change in their spirit, of which it is difficult to foresee the bounds. Not that the men who now hold the ancestral view will, as a rule, exchange it for the view of the Vatican; but that, as in the course of nature they depart, Vaticanists will grow up, and take their places.

The first official head of the Anglo-Roman body in England was the wise and loyal Archpriest Blackwell. He was deposed by the Pope in 1608, " chiefly, it is supposed, for his advocacy of the oath of allegiance,"* which had been devised by King James, in order that he might confer peace and security upon loyal Roman Catholics.† Bellarmine denounced, as heretical, its denial of the power of the Pope to depose the king, and release his subjects from their allegiance. Pope Paul V. condemned the oath by a brief in October, 1606. The unfortunate members of his communion could not believe this brief to be authentic.‡ So a second brief was sent in September, 1607, to confirm and enforce the first. Blackwell gallantly advised his

---

* Butler, 'Historical Memoirs,' iii. 411.
† *Ibid.* i. 303, *seq.*   ‡ *Ibid.* 317.

flock to take the oath in defiance of the brief. Priests confined in Newgate petitioned the Pope to have compassion on them. Forty-eight doctors of the Sorbonne against six, declared that it might be taken with good conscience. And taken it was by many; but taken in despite of the tyrannical injunctions of Paul V., unhappily confirmed by Urban VIII. and by Innocent X.*

When it was proposed, in 1648, to banish Roman Catholics on account of the deposing power, their divines met and renounced the doctrine. This renunciation was condemned at Rome as heretical; but the attitude of France on these questions at the time prevented the publication of the decree.†

When the loyal remonstrance of 1661 had been signed by certain Bishops and others of Ireland, it was condemned at Rome, in July 1662, by the Congregation *de propagandâ*; and in the same month the Papal Nuncio at Brussels, who superintended the concerns of Irish Roman Catholics at the time, denounced it as already condemned by the constitutions of Paul V. and Innocent X.; and specially censured the ecclesiastics who, by signing it, had misled the laity.‡

Well may Butler say, "The claim of the Popes to temporal power, by Divine right, has been one of the most calamitous events in the history of the Church. Its effects since the Reformation, on the English and Irish Catholics, have been dreadful." § And again: "How often did our ancestors experience that ultra-catholicism is one of the worst enemies of catholicity!"‖

---

* Butler, i. 352.
† Caron, 'Remonstrantia Hibernorum.' Ed. 1731, p. 7. Comp. Butler, 'Hist. Memoirs,' ii. 18.
‡ Caron, p. 4. Butler, ii. 401, 402.
§ Butler, i. 192. ‖ *Ibid.* ii. 85; also ii. 20.

The vigour of the mind of Dryden is nowhere more evident than in parts of his poems of controversial theology; and they are important, as exhibiting that view of Roman Catholic tenets, which was presented at the time for the purposes of proselytism. He mentions various opinions as to the seat of infallibility, describing that of the Pope's infallibility, with others, as held by "some doctors," and states what he considers to be the true doctrine of the Latin Church, as follows:—

> " I then affirm, that this unfailing guide
> In Pope and general councils must reside,
> Both lawful, both combined : what one decrees,
> By numerous votes, the other ratifies :
> On this undoubted sense the Church relies."*

When, in 1682, the Gallican Church, by the first of its four Articles, rejected the sophistical distinction of direct and indirect authority, and absolutely denied the power of the Pope in temporals, to this article, says Butler, there was hardly a dissentient voice either clerical or lay. He adds that this principle is " now adopted by the universal Catholic Church."†

Such was the sad condition of the Anglo-Roman body in the seventeenth century. They were ground between the demands of the civil power, stern, but substantially just, on the one hand, and the cruel and outrageous impositions of the Court of Rome on the other. Even for the shameful scenes associated with the name and time of Titus Oates, that Court is largely responsible : and the spirit that governed it in regard to the oath of Allegiance is the very same spirit, which gained its latest triumphs in the Council of the Vatican.

---

* 'The Hind and Panther,' part ii.
† Butler, i. 358, and ii. 20.

I now pass to the period, which followed the Revolution of 1688, especially with reference to the bold assertion that before 1870 the Pope's infallibility was a doctrine of Divine faith.

The Revolution, brought about by invasions of the law and the constitution, with which the Church of Rome was disastrously associated, necessarily partook of a somewhat vindictive character as towards the Anglo-Roman body. Our penal provisions were a mitigated, but also a debased, copy of the Papal enactments against heresy. It was not until 1757, on the appointment of the Duke of Bedford to the Lord-Lieutenancy of Ireland, that the first sign of life was given.* Indeed it was only in 1756 that a new penal law had been proposed in Ireland.† But, in the next year, the Irish Roman Catholic Committee published a Declaration which disavowed the deposing and absolving power, with other odious opinions. Here it was averred that the Pope had "no temporal or civil jurisdiction," "directly or indirectly, within this realm." And it was also averred that it "is not an article of the Catholic faith, neither are we thereby required to believe or profess that the Pope is infallible": in diametrical contradiction to the declaration of Archbishop Manning, that persons of his religion were bound to this belief before the Council of 1870.‡

It may, indeed, be observed that in declaring they are not required to believe the infallibility of the Pope, the subscribers to this document do not say anything to show

---

* Butler, iv. 511. Sir H. Parnell, 'History of the Penal Laws.'

† Madden, 'Historical Notice of the Penal Laws,' p. 8.

‡ I cite the terms of this document from 'The Elector's Guide,' addressed to the freeholders of the county of York. No. 1, p. 44. York, 1826. It is also, I believe, to be found in Parnell's 'History of the Penal Laws,' 1808.

that they did not for themselves hold the tenet. But a brief explanation will show that the distinction in this case is little better than futile. As we have seen, the Declaration set forth that the Pope had no temporal power in England. Now, in the notorious Bull, *Unam Sanctam*, it had been positively declared *ex cathedrâ* that both the temporal and the spiritual sword were at the command of the Church, and that it was the office of the Pope, by a power not human but Divine, to judge and correct the secular authority. The language of the Declaration of 1757 was directly at variance with the language of the Pope, speaking *ex cathedrâ*, and therefore here if anywhere infallible. It could, therefore, only have been consistently used by persons, who for themselves did not accept the tenet. I am aware it will be argued that the infallible part of the Bull is only the last sentence. It is well for those who so teach that Boniface VIII. is not alive to hear them. The last sentence is introduced by the word " Porro," *furthermore:* a strange substitute for " Be it enacted." The true force of that sentence seems to be : " Furthermore we declare that this subjection to the Roman Pontiff, as hereinbefore described, is to be held as necessary for salvation." It is not the substance ; but an addition to the substance.

If, however, anything had been wanting in this Declaration, it would have been abundantly supplied by the Protestation of the Roman Catholics of England in 1788–9. In this very important document, which brought about the passing of the great English Relief Act of 1791, besides a repetition of the assurances generally, which had been theretofore conveyed, there are contained statements of the greatest significance.

1. That the subscribers to it " acknowledge no infallibility in the Pope."

2. That their Church has no power that can directly or indirectly injure Protestants, as all she can do is to refuse them her sacraments, which they do not want.

3. That no ecclesiastical power whatever can "directly or indirectly affect or interfere with the independence, sovereignty, laws, constitution, or government," of the realm.

This Protestation was, in the strictest sense, a representative and binding document. It was signed by two hundred and forty-one priests,* including all the Vicars Apostolic: by all the clergy and laity in England of any note; and in 1789, at a general meeting of the English Catholics in London, it was subscribed by every person present.†

Thus we have on the part of the entire body, of which Archbishop Manning is now the head,‡ a direct, literal, and unconditional rejection of the cardinal tenet which he tells us has always been believed by his Church, and was an article of Divine faith before as well as after 1870. Nor was it merely that the Protestation and the Relief coincided in time. The protesters explicitly set forth that the penal laws against them were founded on the doctrines imputed

---

* Slater's Letters on 'Roman Catholic Tenets,' p. 6.

† Butler, 'Hist. Memoirs,' ii. 118, 126.

‡ Prelates really should remember that they may lead their trustful lay followers into strange predicaments. Thus Mr. Towneley (of Towneley, I believe), in his letter of Nov. 18 to the 'Times,' dwells, I have no doubt with perfect justice, on the loyalty of his ancestors; but, unhappily, goes on to assert that "the Catholic Church has always held and taught the infallibility of the Pope in matters of faith and morals." No: the Roman Catholics of England denied it in their [Protestation of 1788-9; and on the list of the Committee, which prepared and promoted that Protestation, I find the name of Peregrine Towneley, of Towneley.—*Ibid.* ii. 304.

to them, and they asked and obtained the relief on the express ground that they renounced and condemned the doctrines.*

Some objection seems to have been taken at Rome to a portion (we are not told what) of the terms of the Protestation. The history connected herewith is rather obscurely given in Butler. But the Protestation itself was, while the Bill was before Parliament, deposited in the British Museum, by order of the Anglo-Roman body: "that it may be preserved there as a lasting memorial of their political and moral integrity."† Two of the four Vicars Apostolic, two clergymen, and one layman, withdrew their names from the Protestation on the deposit; all the rest of the signatures remained.

Canon Flanagan's 'History of the Church in England' impugns the representative character of the Committee, and declares that the Court of Rome approved of proceedings taken in opposition to it.‡ But the material fact is the subscription of the Protestation by the clergy and laity at large. On this subject he admits that it was signed by "the greater part of both clergy and laity";§ and states that an organisation in opposition to the Committee, founded in 1794 by one of the Vicars Apostolic, died a natural death after "a very few years." ‖ The most significant part of the case, however, is perhaps this: that the work of Flanagan, which aims at giving a tinge of the new historical colour to the opinions of the Anglo-Roman body, was not published until 1857, when things had taken an altogether new direction, and when the Emancipation controversies had been long at rest.

---

* Butler, 'Hist. Memoirs,' ii. 119, 125. † *Ibid.* ii. 136–8.
‡ Flanagan, ii. 398.   § *Ibid.* ii. 394.
‖ *Ibid.* ii. 407.

The Act of 1791 for England was followed by that of 1793 for Ireland. The Oath inserted in this Act is founded upon the Declaration of 1757, and embodies a large portion of it, including the words:—

"It is not an article of the Catholic Faith, neither am I thereby required to believe or profess, that the Pope is infallible."

I refer to this oath, not because I attach an especial value to that class of security, but because we now come to a Synodical Declaration of the Irish Bishops, which constitutes perhaps the most salient point of the whole of this singular history.

On the 26th of February, 1810, those Bishops declared as follows:—

"That said Oath, and the promises, declarations, abjurations, and protestations therein contained are, *notoriously, to the Roman Catholic Church at large, become a part of the Roman Catholic religion, as taught by us the Bishops, and received and maintained by the Roman Catholic Churches in Ireland; and as such are approved and sanctioned by the other Roman Catholic Churches.*" *

Finally: it will scarcely be denied that Bishop Baines was, to say the least, a very eminent and representative member of the Anglo-Roman body. In 1822, he wrote as follows:—

"Bellarmine, and some other Divines, chiefly Italians, have believed the Pope infallible, when proposing *ex cathedrâ* an article of faith. *But in England or Ireland I do not believe that any Catholic maintains the infallibility of the Pope.*" †

It will now, I think, have sufficiently appeared to the reader who has followed this narration, how mildly, I may say how inadequately, I have set forth in my former tract the pledges which were given by the authorities of the Roman Catholic Church to the Crown and State of the

---

* Slater on 'Roman Catholic Tenets,' pp. 14, 15.
† Defence against Dr. Moysey, p. 230, 1822.

United Kingdom, and by means of which principally they obtained the remission of the penal laws, and admission to full civil equality. We were told in England by the Anglo-Roman Bishops, clergy, and laity, that they rejected the tenet of the Pope's infallibility. We were told in Ireland that they rejected the doctrine of the Pope's temporal power, whether direct or indirect, although the Pope had in the most solemn and formal manner asserted his possession of it. We were also told in Ireland that Papal infallibility was no part of the Roman Catholic faith, and never could be made a part of it: and that the impossibility of incorporating it in their religion was notorious to the Roman Catholic Church at large, and was become part of their religion, and this not only in Ireland, but throughout the world. These are the declarations, which reach in effect from 1661 to 1810; and it is in the light of these declarations that the evidence of Dr. Doyle in 1825, and the declarations of the English and Irish prelates of the Papal communion shortly afterwards, are to be read. Here, then, is an extraordinary fulness and clearness of evidence, reaching over nearly two centuries: given by and on behalf of millions of men: given in documents patent to all the world: perfectly well known to the See and Court of Rome, as we know expressly with respect to nearly the most important of all these assurances, namely, the actual and direct repudiation of infallibility in 1788–9. So that either that See and Court had at the last-named date, and at the date of the Synod of 1810, abandoned the dream of enforcing infallibility on the Church, or else by wilful silence they were guilty of practising upon the British Crown one of the blackest frauds recorded in history.

The difficulties now before us were fully foreseen during

the sittings of the Council of 1870. In the Address prepared by Archbishop Kenrick, of St. Louis, but not delivered, because a stop was put to the debate, I find these words :—

"Quomodo fides sic gubernio Anglicano data conciliari possit cum definitione papalis infallibilitatis . . . ipsi viderint qui ex Episcopis Hibernicnsibus, sicut ego ipse, illud juramentum præstiterint."*

"In what way the pledge thus given to the English Government can be reconciled with the definition of Papal infallibility let those of the Irish Bishops consider, who, like myself, have taken the oath in question."

The oath was, I presume, that of 1793. However, in Friedberg's 'Sammlung der Actenstücke zum Concil,' p. 151 (Tübingen, 1872), I find it stated, I hope untruly, that the 'Civiltà Cattolica,' the prime favourite of Vaticanism, in Series viii. vol. i. p. 730, announced, among those who had submitted to the Definition, the name of Archbishop Kenrick.

Let it not, however, be for a moment supposed that I mean to charge upon those who gave the assurances of 1661, of 1757, of 1783, of 1793, of 1810, of 1825-6, the guilt of falsehood. I have not a doubt that what they said, they one and all believed. It is for Archbishop Manning and his confederates, not for me, to explain how these things have come about; or it is for Archbishop MacHale, who joined as a Bishop in the assurances of 1826, and who then stood in the shadow and recent recollection of the Synod of 1810, but who now is understood to have become a party, by promulgation, to the Decree of the Pope's infallibility. There are but two alternatives to choose between : on the one side, that which I reject, the hypothesis of sheer perjury and falsehood;

---

* Friedrich, 'Doc. ad Illust. Conc. Vat.,' i. 219.

on the other, that policy of "violence and change in faith" which I charged, and stirred so much wrath by charging, in my former tract. I believed, and I still believe it to be the true, as well as the milder, explanation. It is for those who reject it to explain their preference for the other solution of this most curious problem of history.*

And now what shall we say to that colouring power of imagination with which Dr. Newman† tints the wide landscape of these most intractable facts, when he says it is a pity the Bishops could not have anticipated the likelihood that in 1870 the Council of the Vatican would attach to the Christian creed the Article of the Pope's infallibility? A pity it may be; but it surely is not a wonder: because they told us, as a fact notorious to themselves and to the whole Roman Catholic world, that the passing of such a decree was impossible.‡ Let us reserve our faculty of wondering for the letter of an Anglo-Roman, or if he prefers it, Romano-Anglian Bishop, who in a published circular presumes to term "scandalous" the letter of an English gentleman, because in that letter he had declared he still held the belief which, in 1788-9, the whole body of the Roman Catholics of England assured Mr. Pitt that they held;§ and let us learn which of the resources of theological skill will avail to bring together these innovations and the *semper eadem* of which I am, I fear, but writing the lamentable epitaph.

"Non bene conveniunt, nec in una sede morantur."

---

* See Appendices D and E.
† Dr. Newman, p. 17. ‡ See Appendix D.
§ Letter of Mr. Petre to the 'Times' of Nov. 15, 1874; of Bishop Vaughan, Jan. 2, 1875. ‖ Ov. Metamorph.

This question has been raised by me primarily as a British question; and I hope that, so far as this country is concerned, I have now done something to throw light upon the question whether Papal infallibility was or was not matter of Divine Faith before 1870; and consequently on the question whether the Vatican Decrees have "in no jot or tittle" altered the conditions of civil allegiance in connection with this infallibility.*

The declaration of the Irish prelates in 1810 was a full assurance to us that what they asserted for their country was also asserted for the whole Romish world.

But as evidence has been produced which goes directly into antiquity, and arguments have been made to show how innocuous is the new-fangled form of religion, I proceed to deal with such evidence and argument, in regard to my twofold contention against the Decrees—

1. In respect to infallibility.
2. In respect to obedience.

---

* For a practical indication of the effect produced by the Roman Catholic disclaimers, now denounced as "scandalous," see Appendix E.

IV. THE VATICAN COUNCIL AND THE INFALLIBILITY OF THE POPE, CONTINUED.

Breach with History, No. 2.

IN a single instance, I have to express my regret for a statement made with culpable inadvertence. It is in p. 28, where I have stated that the Popes had kept up their claim to dogmatic infallibility with comparatively little intermission " for well-nigh one thousand years." I cannot even account for so loose an assertion, except by the fact that the point lay out of the main line of my argument, and thus the slip of the pen once made escaped correction. Of the claim to a supremacy virtually absolute, which I combined with the other claim, the statement is true ; for this may be carried back, perhaps, to the ninth century and the appearance of the false decretals. That was the point, which entered so largely into the great conflicts of the Middle Ages. It is the point which I have treated as the more momentous ; and the importance of the tenet of infallibility in faith and morals seems to me to arise chiefly from its aptitude for combination with the other. As matter of fact, the stability, and great authority, of the Roman Church in controversies of faith were acknowledged generally from an early period. But the heresy of Honorius, to say nothing of other Popes, became, from his condemnation by a General Council and by a long series of Popes as well as by other Councils, a matter so notorious, that it could not fade from the view even of the darkest age ; and the possibility of an heretical Pope grew to be an idea perfectly familiar to the general mind of Christendom. Hence in the Bull, *Cum ex Apostolatûs*

Officio, Paul IV. declares (1559), that if a heretic is chosen as Pope, all his acts shall be void *ab initio*. All Christians are absolved from their obedience to him, and enjoined to have recourse to the temporal power.* So likewise, in the Decretum of Gratian itself it is provided, that the Pope can only be brought to trial in case he is found to deviate from the faith.†

It is an opinion held by great authorities, that no pontiff before Leo X. attempted to set up the infallibility of Popes as a dogma. Of the citations in its favour which are arrayed by Archbishop Manning in his *Privilegium Petri*,‡ I do not perceive any earlier than the thirteenth century, which appear so much as to bear upon the question. There is no Conciliary declaration, as I need scarcely add, of the doctrine. This being so, the point is not of primary importance. The claim is one thing, its adoption by the Church, and the interlacing of it with a like adoption of the claim to obedience, are another. I do not deny to the opinion of Papal infallibility an active, though a chequered and intermittent, life exceeding six centuries.

Since, then, I admit that for so long a time the influences now triumphant in the Roman Church have been directed towards the end they have at last attained, and seeing that my statement as to the liberty which prevailed before 1870 has been impugned, I am bound to offer some proof of that statement. I will proceed, in this instance as in others, by showing that my allegation

---

* Schulte, 'Power of the Popes,' iv. 30.

† "Hujus culpas istic redarguere præsumit mortalium nullus, quia cunctos ipse judicaturus a nemine est judicandus, *nisi deprehendatur a fide devius*."—Decr. i. Dist. xl. c. vi.

‡ 'Petri Privilegium,' ii. 70-91.

is much within the truth : that not only had the Latin Church forborne to adopt the tenet of Papal infallibility, but that she was rather bound by consistency with her own principles, as recorded in history, to repel and repudiate that tenet. I refer to the events of the great epoch marked by the Council of Constance. And the proof of the state of facts with regard to that epoch will also be proof of my more general allegation that the Church of Rome does not keep good faith with history, as it is handed down to her, and marked out for her, by her own annals. I avoided this discussion in the former tract, because it is necessarily tinctured with theology : but the denial is a challenge, which I cannot refuse to take up.

It is alleged that certain of my assertions may be left to confute one another. I will show that they are perfectly consistent with one another.

The first of them charged on Vaticanism that it had disinterred and brought into action the extravagant claims of Papal authority, which were advanced by Popes at the climax of their power, but which never entered into the faith even of the Latin Church.

The second, that it had added two if not three new articles to the Christian Creed; the two articles of the Immaculate Conception, and of Papal Infallibility; with what is at least a new law of Christian obligation, the absolute duty of all Christians and all Councils to obey the Pope in his decrees and commands, even where fallible, over the whole domain of faith, morals, and the government and discipline of the Church. This law is now for the first time, I believe, laid down by the joint and infallible authority of Pope and council. Dr. Newman*

---

* Dr. Newman, pp. 45, 53.

wonders that I should call the law absolute. I call it absolute, because it is without exception, and without limitation.

To revive obsolete claims to authority, and to innovate in matter of belief, are things perfectly compatible : we have seen them disastrously combined. In such innovation is involved, as I will now show, a daring breach with history.

While one portion of the Roman theologians have held the infallibility of the Pope, many others have taught that an Ecumenical Council together with a Pope constitutes *per se* an infallible authority in faith and morals. I believe it to be also true that it was, down to that disastrous date, compatible with Roman orthodoxy to hold that not even a Pope and a Council united could give the final seal of certainty to a definition, and that for this end there was further necessary the sanction, by acceptance, of the Church diffused. This last opinion, however, seems to have gone quite out of fashion; and I now address myself to the position in argument of those who hold that in the decree of a Council, approved by the Pope, the character of infallibility resides.

Both the Council of Constance and the Council of the Vatican were in the Roman sense Œcumenical : and it is this class of councils alone that is meant, where infallibility is treated of. I shall endeavour to be brief, and to use the simplest language.

The Council of the Vatican decreed (chap. iii.) that the Pope had from Christ immediate power over the universal Church (par. ii.).

That all were bound to obey him, of whatever rite and dignity, collectively as well as individually (*cujuscunque ritûs et dignitatis . . . tam seorsum singuli, quam simul omnes.* Ibid.)

That this duty of obedience extended to all matters of

faith, of morals, and of the discipline and government of the Church (*ibid.*, and par. iv.).

That in all ecclesiastical causes he is judge, without appeal, or possibility of reversal (par. iv.).

That the definitions of the Pope in faith and morals, delivered *ex cathedrâ*, are irreformable, *ex sese, non autem ex consensu Ecclesiæ*, and are invested with the infallibility granted by Christ in the said subject matter to the Church (ch. iv.).

Now let us turn to the Council of Constance.

This Council, supported by the following Council of Basle before its translation to Ferrara, had decreed in explicit terms that it had from Christ immediate power over the universal Church, of which it was the representative.

That all were bound to obey it, of whatever state and dignity, even if Papal, in all matters pertaining to faith, or to the extirpation of the subsisting schism, or to the reformation of the Church in its head and its members.*

In conformity herewith, the Council of Constance cited, as being itself a superior authority, three Popes to its bar. Gregory XII. anticipated his sentence by resignation. Benedict XIII. was deposed, as was John XXIII., for divers crimes and offences, but not for heresy. Having thus made void the Papal Chair, the Council made the provisions, under which Pope Martin V. was elected.

It is not my object to attempt a general appreciation of the Council of Constance. There is much against it to be said from many points of view, if there be more for it. But I point out that, for the matter now in hand, the questions of fact are clear, and that its decrees are in flat and diametrical contradiction to those of the Vatican.

---

* Labbe, 'Concilia,' xii. 22, ed. Paris, 1672.

This of itself would not constitute any difficulty for Roman theology, and would give no proof of its breach with history. It is admitted on all or nearly all hands that a Council, however great its authority may be, is not of itself infallible. What really involves a fatal breach with history is, when a body, which professes to appeal to it, having proclaimed a certain organ to be infallible, then proceeds to ascribe to it to-day an utterance contradictory to its utterance of yesterday; and, thus depriving it not only of all certainty, but of all confidence, lays its honour prostrate in the dust. This can only be brought home to the Roman Church, if two of her Councils, contradicting one another in the subject matter of faith or morals, have each respectively been confirmed by the Pope, and have thus obtained, in Roman eyes, the stamp of infallibility. Now this is what I charge in the present instance.

It is not disputed, but loudly asseverated, by Vaticanists, that the Council of the Vatican has been approved and confirmed by the Pope.

But an allegation has been set up that the Council of Constance did not receive that confirmation in respect to the Decree of the Fifth Session which asserted its power, given by Christ, over the Pope. Bishop Ullathorne says :—

"Although the mode of proceeding in that Council was really informal, inasmuch as its members voted by nations, a portion of its doctrinal decrees obtained force through the dogmatic Constitution of Martin V."*

Here it is plainly implied that the Decree of the Fifth Session was not confirmed. And I have read in some Ultramontane production of the last three months an exulting observation, that the Decrees of the Fourth and Fifth Sessions were not confirmed by the Pope, and that

---

* 'Expostulation Unravelled,' p. 42.

thus, I presume like the smitten fig-tree, they have remained a dead letter. Let us examine this allegation; but not that other statement of Archbishop Manning that the proceeding was null from the nullity of the assembly, the irregularity of the voting, and the heterodoxy of the matter.* The Pope's confirmation covers and disposes of all these arbitrary pleas. Whether it was given or not, is to be tried by the evidence of authoritative documents.

In the record of the Council of Constance we are told that, in its Forty-fifth Session, the Pope declared not that he confirmed a part of its doctrinal decrees, but "that he would hold and inviolably observe, and never counteract in any manner, each and all of the things which the Council had in full assembly determined, concluded, and decreed in matters of faith (*in materiis fidei*)." † And he approves and ratifies accordingly.

Embracing all the decrees described in its scope, this declaration is in tone as much an adhesion, as a confirmation by independent or superior authority. But let that pass. Evidently it gives all that the Pope had in his power to give.

The only remaining question is, whether the Decree of the Fifth Session was, or was not, a decree of faith?

Now upon this question there are at least two independent lines of argument, each of which respectively and separately, is fatal to the Ultramontane contention: this contention being that, for want of the confirmation of Pope Martin V., that Decree fell to the ground.

First; Pope Martin V. derived his whole power to

---

* 'Petri Privilegium,' ii. 95.

† Labbe, 'Concilia,' xii. 258. See Appendix F for the most important passages.

confirm from his election to the Papal Chair by the Council. And the Council was competent to elect, because the See was vacant. And the See was vacant, because of the depositions of two rival Popes, and the resignation of the third; for if the See was truly vacant before, there had been no Pope since the schism in 1378, which is not supposed by either side. But the power of the Council to vacate the See was in virtue of the principle asserted by the Decree of the Fifth Session. We arrive then at the following dilemma. Either that Decree had full validity by the confirmation of the Pope, or Martin the Fifth was not a Pope; the Cardinals made or confirmed by him were not Cardinals, and could not elect validly his successor, Eugenius IV.; so that the Papal succession has failed since an early date in the fifteenth century, or more than four hundred and fifty years ago.

Therefore the Decree of the Fifth Session must, upon Roman principles, have been included in the *materiæ fidei* determined by the Council, and, accordingly, in the confirmation by Pope Martin V.

But again. It has been held by some Roman writers that Pope Martin V. only confirmed the Decrees touching Faith; that the Decree of the Fifth Session did not touch Faith, but only Church-government, and that accordingly it remained unconfirmed.

Now in the Apostles' Creed, and in the Nicene Creed, we all express belief in the Holy Catholic Church. Its institution and existence are therefore strictly matter of faith. How can it be reasonably contended, that the organised body is an article of faith, but that the seat of its vital, sovereign power, by and from which it becomes operative for belief and conduct, belongs to the inferior region of the ever mutable discipline of the Church?

But this is argument only; and we have a more sure criterion at command, which will convict Vaticanism for the present purpose out of its own mouth. Vaticanism has effectually settled this question as against itself. For it has declared that the Papal Infallibility is a dogma of Faith (*divinitus revelatum dogma*, 'Const.' ch. iv.). But if by this definition, the Infallibility of the Pope in definitions of faith belongs to the province of *materiæ fidei* and of *ea quæ pertinent ad fidem*, the negative of the proposition thus affirmed, being in the same subject-matter, belongs to the same province. It therefore seems to follow, by a demonstration perfectly rigorous,—

1. That Pope Martin V. confirmed (or adopted) a Decree, which declares the judgments and proceedings of the Pope, in matters of faith, without exception, to be reformable, and therefore fallible.

2. That Pope Pius IX. confirmed (and proposed) a Decree, which declares certain judgments of the Pope, in matters of faith and morals, to be infallible; and these, with his other judgments in faith, morals, and the discipline and government of the Church, to be irreformable.

3. That the new oracle contradicts the old, and again the Roman Church has broken with history in contradicting itself.

4. That no oracle, which contradicts itself, is an infallible oracle.

5. That a so-called Œcumenical Council of the Roman Church, confirmed or non-confirmed by the Pope, has, upon its own showing, no valid claim to infallible authority.

The gigantic forgeries of the false Decretals, the general contempt of Vaticanism for history, are subjects far too wide for me to touch. But for the present I leave my assertion in this matter to stand upon—

1. The case of the Roman Catholics of the United Kingdom before 1829.

2. The Decrees of the Council of Constance, compared with the Decrees of the Council of the Vatican.

When these assertions are disposed of, it will be time enough to place others in the rank. I will now say a word on the cognate subject of Gallicanism, which has also been brought upon the *tapis*.

It would be unreasonable to expect from Archbishop Manning greater accuracy in his account of a foreign Church, than he has exhibited with regard to the history of the communion over which he energetically presides.

As the most famous and distinct of its manifestations was that exhibited in the Four Articles of 1682, it has pleased the Archbishop to imagine, and imagining to state, that in that year Gallicanism took its rise. Even with the help of this airy supposition, he has to admit that in the Church where all is unity, certainty, and authority, a doctrine contrary to Divine faith, yet proclaimed by the Church of France, was, for want of a General Council, tolerated for one hundred and eighty-eight years. Indeed, he alleges[*] the errors of the Council of Constance, four hundred and sixty years ago, as a reason for the Council of the Vatican.

"Nor were Catholics free to deny his infallibility before 1870. The denial of his infallibility had indeed never been condemned by a definition, because *since the rise of Gallicanism in* 1682 no Œcumenical Council had ever been convoked."[†]

I will not stop to inquire why, if the Pope has all this

---

[*] 'Petri Privilegium,' ii. 40.
[†] Letter to 'Macmillan's Magazine,' Oct. 22, 1874.

time been infallible, a Council was necessary for the issuing of a definition; since we are now on matters of history, and the real difficulty would be to know where to dip into the prior history of France without finding matter in utter contradiction to the Archbishop's allegation. An Anglo-Roman writer has told us that in the year 1612 [query 1614?] the assembly of the Gallican Church declared that the power of the Popes related to spiritual matters and eternal life, not to civil concerns and temporal possessions.* In the year 1591, at Mantes and Chartres, the prelates of France in their assembly refused the order of the Pope to quit the king, and on the 21st of September repudiated his Bulls, as being null in substance and in form.† It has always been understood that the French Church played a great part in the Council of Constance: is this also to be read backwards, or effaced from the records? Or, to go a little further back, the Council of Paris in 1393 withdrew its obedience altogether from Benedict XIII., without transferring it to his rival at Rome: restored it upon conditions in 1403; again withdrew it, because the conditions had not been fulfilled, in 1406: and so remained until the Council of Constance and the election of Martin V.‡ And what are we to say to Fleury? who writes:

'Le concile de Constance établit la maxime *de tout temps enseignée en France*, que tout Pape est soumis au jugement de tout concile universel en ce qui concerne la foi." §

---

* Cited in Slater's Letters, p. 23, from Hook's 'Principia,' iii. 577.
† Continuator of Fleury, 'Hist. Eccl.,' xxxvi. 337 (Book 169, ch. 84).
‡ Du Chastenet, 'Nouvelle Histoire du Concile de Constance' (preface); and 'Preuves,' pp. 79, 84, *seq.*, 95, 479 (Paris, 1718).
§ Fleury, 'Nouv. Opusc.,' p. 44, cited in Demaistre, 'Du Pape,' p. 82. See also Fleury, 'Hist. Eccl.' (Book 102, ch. 188).

One of the four articles of 1682 simply reaffirms the decree of Constance : and as Archbishop Manning has been the first, so he will probably be the last person to assert, that Gallicanism took its rise in 1682.

This is not the place to show how largely, if less distinctly, the spirit of what are called the Gallican liberties entered into the ideas and institutions of England, Germany, and even Spain. Neither will I dwell on the manner in which the decrees of Constance ruled for a time not only the minds of a school or party, but the policy of the Western Church at large, were confirmed and repeatedly renewed by the succeeding Council of Basle, and proved their efficacy and sway by the remarkable submission of Eugenius IV. to that Council. But I will cite the single sentence in which Mr. Hallam, writing, alas, nearly sixty years back, has summed up the case of the decrees of Constance.

"These decrees are the great pillars of that moderate theory with respect to the Papal authority, which distinguished the Gallican Church, and is embraced, I presume, by almost all laymen, and the major part of ecclesiastics, on this side the Alps." *

* 'Hist. of the Middle Ages,' chap. vii. part 2.

V. THE VATICAN COUNCIL AND OBEDIENCE TO THE POPE.

ARCHBISHOP MANNING has boldly grappled with my proposition that the Third Chapter of the Vatican Decrees had forged new chains for the Christian people, in regard to obedience, by giving its authority to what was previously a claim of the Popes only, and so making it a claim of the Church. He is astonished at the statement: and he offers* what he thinks a sufficient confutation of it, in six citations.

The four last begin with Innocent III., and end with the Council of Trent. Two, from Innocent III. and Sixtus IV., simply claim the *regimen*, or government of the Church, which no one denies them. The Council of Florence speaks of *plena potestas*, and the Council of Trent of *suprema potestas*, as belonging to the Pope. Neither of these assertions touches the point. Full power, and supreme power, in the government of a body, may still be limited by law. No other power can be above them. But it does not follow that they can command from all persons an unconditional obedience, unless themselves empowered by law so to do. We are familiar, under the British monarchy, both with the term supreme, and with its limitation.

The Archbishop, however, quotes a Canon or Chapter of a Roman Council in 863, which anathematises all who despise the Pope's orders with much breadth and amplitude of phrase. If taken without the context, it fully covers the ground taken by the Vatican Council. It anathematises

---

* Archbishop Manning, pp. 12, 13.

all who contemn the decrees of the Roman See in faith, discipline, or correction of manners, or for the remedy or prevention of mischief. Considering that the four previous Canons of this Council, and the whole proceedings, relate entirely to the case of the Divorce of Lothair, it might, perhaps, be argued that the whole constitute only a *privilegium*, or law for the individual case, and that the anathema of the Fifth Canon must be limited to those who set at nought the Pope's proceedings in that case. But the point is of small consequence to my argument.

But then the Roman Council is local; and adds no very potent reinforcement to the sole authority of the Pope. The question then remains how to secure for this local and Papal injunction the sanction of the Universal Church, in the Roman sense of the word. Archbishop Manning, perfectly sensible of what is required of him, writes that " this Canon was recognised in the Eighth General Council, held at Constantinople in 869." He is then more than contented with this array of proofs; and, confining himself, as I am bound to say he does, in all personal matters throughout his work, to the mildest language consistent with the full expression of his ideas, he observes that I am manifestly out of my depth.*

I know not the exact theological value of the term " recognised"; but I conceive it to mean virtual adoption. Such an adoption of such a claim by a General Council, appeared to me a fact of the utmost significance. I referred to many of the historians of the Church: but I found no notice of it in those whom I consulted, including Baronius. From these unproductive references I went onwards to the original documents.

---

* Archbishop Manning, 'Vatican Decrees,' pp. 12, 13.

The Eighth General Council, so-called, comprised only those Bishops of the East who adhered to, and were supported by, the See of Rome and the Patriarch Ignatius, in the great conflict of the ninth century. It would not, therefore, have been surprising if its canons had given some at least equivocal sanction to the high Papal claims. But, on the contrary, they may be read with the greatest interest as showing, at the time immediately bordering on the publication of the false Decretals, how little way those claims had made in the general body of the Church. The system which they describe is the Patriarchal, not the Papal system: the fivefold distribution of the Christian Church under the five great Sees of the Elder and the New Rome, Alexandria, Antioch, and Jerusalem. Of these the Pope of Rome is the first, but as *primus inter pares* (Canons XVII., XXI., Lat.).* The causes of clergy on appeal are to be finally decided by the Patriarch in each Patriarchate (Canon XXVI., Lat.) :† and it is declared that any General Council has authority to deal, but should deal respectfully, with controversies of or touching the Roman Church itself (Canon XXI. Lat., XIII. Gr.)‡ This is one of the Councils which solemnly anathematises Pope Honorius as a heretic.

The reference made by Archbishop Manning is, as he has had the goodness to inform me, to the Second Canon.§ The material words are these:—

"Regarding the most blessed Pope Nicholas as an organ of the Holy Spirit, and likewise his most holy successor Adrian, we accordingly

---

* Labbe (ed. Paris, 1671), vol. x. pp. 1136, 1140.
† *Ibid.* 1143.
‡ *Ibid.* 1140, 1375.
§ *Ibid.* p. 1127 Lat., p. 1367 Gr.; where the reader should be on his guard against the Latin version, and look to the Greek original.

define and enact that all which they have set out and promulgated synodically, from time to time, as well for the defence and well-being of the Church of Constantinople, and of its Chief Priest and most holy Patriarch Ignatius, as likewise for the expulsion and condemnation of Photius, neophyte and intruder, be always observed and kept alike entire and untouched, under (or according to) the heads set forth (*cum expositis capitulis*)." *

There is not in the Canon anything relating to the Popes generally, but only to two particular Popes; nor any reference to what they did personally, but only to what they did synodically; nor to what they did synodically in all matters, but only in the controversy with Photius and the Eastern Bishops adhering to him. There is not one word relating to the Canon of 863, or to the Council which passed it: which was a Council having nothing to do with the Photian controversy, but called for the purpose of supporting Pope Nicholas I. in what is commonly deemed his righteous policy with respect to the important case of the Divorce of Lothair.†

So that the demonstration of the Archbishop falls wholly to the ground: and down to this time my statement remains entire and unhurt. The matter contained in it will remain very important until the Council or the Pope shall amend its decree so as to bring it into conformity with the views of Dr. Newman, and provide a relief to the private conscience by opening in the great gate of Obedience a little wicket-door of exceptions for those who are minded to disobey.

Had the Decrees of 1870 been in force in the sixteenth and seventeenth centuries, Roman Catholic peers could not have done what, until the reign of Charles II., they did; could not have made their way to the House of Lords

---

* See the original in Appendix G.
† Labbe, x. 766 *sqq.*

by taking the oath of allegiance, despite the Pope's command. But that is not all. The Pope *ex cathedrâ* had bidden the Roman Catholics of England in the eighteenth century, and in the sixteenth, and from the fourteenth, to believe in the Deposing power as an article of faith. But they rejected it: and no unquestioned law of their Church forbade them to reject it. Are they not forbidden now? The Pope in the sixteenth century bade the Roman Catholics of England assist the invasion of the Spanish Armada. They disobeyed him. The highest law of their Church left them free to disobey. Are they as free now? That they will assert this freedom for themselves I do not question, nay, I sanguinely believe. From every standing-point, except that of Vaticanism, their title to it is perfect. With Vaticanism to supply their premiss, how are they to conclude? Dr. Newman says there are exceptions to this precept of obedience. But this is just what the Council has not said. The Church by the Council imposes Aye. The private conscience reserves to itself the title to say No. I must confess that in this apology there is to me a strong, undeniable, smack of Protestantism. To reconcile Dr. Newman's conclusion with the premisses of the Vatican will surely require all, if not more than all, "the vigilance, acuteness, and subtlety of the *Schola Theologorum* in its acutest member."*

The days of such proceedings, it is stated, are gone by: and I believe that, in regard to our country, they have passed away beyond recall. But that is not the present question. The present question is whether the right to perform such acts has been effectually disavowed. With this question I now proceed to deal.

---

* Dr. Newman, p. 121.

VI. REVIVED CLAIMS OF THE PAPAL CHAIR.

1. *The Deposing Power.*
2. *The Use of Force.*

It will perhaps have been observed by others, as it has been by me, that from the charges against my account of the Syllabus are notably absent two of its most important and instructive heads. I accuse the Syllabus of teaching the right of the Church to use force, and of maintaining the Deposing power.

When my tract was published, I had little idea of the extent to which, and (as to some of them) the hardihood with which, those who should have confuted my charges would themselves supply evidence to sustain them.

Bishop Clifford, indeed, sustains the deposing power on the ground that it was accorded to the Pope by the nations. It was simply a case like that of the Geneva Arbitrators.* Dr. Newman † defends it, but only upon conditions. The circumstances must be rare and critical. The proceeding must be judicial. It must appeal to the moral law. Lastly, there must be an united consent of various nations. In fine, Dr. Newman accepts the deposing power only under the conditions which, as he thinks, the Pope himself lays down.

These allegations quiet my fears; but they strain my faith; and, purporting to be historical, they shock my judgment. For they are, to speak plainly, without foundation. The Arbitrators at Geneva settled a dispute,

---

* 'Pastoral Letter,' p. 12.
† Dr. Newman, pp. 36, 37.

which, as they recited in formal terms, the two parties to it had empowered and invited them to settle. The point of consent is the only weighty one among the four conditions of Dr. Newman, and is the sole point raised by Bishop Clifford. Did then Paul III., as arbitrator in the case of Henry VIII., pursue a like procedure? The first words of his Bull are, "The condemnation and excommunication of Henry VIII., King of England:" not an auspicious beginning. There is nothing at all about arbitration, or consent of any body, but a solemn and fierce recital of power received from God, not from the nations, or from one nation, or from any fraction of a nation; power "over the nations and over the kingdoms, to pluck up and to destroy, to build up and to plant, as chief over all kings of the whole earth, and all peoples possessing rule." Exactly similar is the "arbitration" of Pius V. between himself and Elizabeth, to the "arbitration" of Paul III. between himself and Henry VIII.

Archbishop Manning, indeed,* has thrown in a statement the utility of which it is hard to understand, that Queen Elizabeth "was baptized a Catholic." She was baptized after Appeals to Rome had been abolished, and two years after the Clergy had owned in the King that title of Headship, which Mary abolished, and which never has been revived. But Archbishop Manning knows quite well that the Papal claims of right extend to all baptized persons whatever, and Queen Victoria could have no exemption unless it could be shown that she was unbaptized.

The doctrine of the consent of nations is a pure imagi-

---

* Archbishop Manning, p. 89. See the Anathemas of the Council of Trent against those who deny that heretics, as being baptized persons, are bound to obedience to the Church. I hope the Archbishop has not incautiously incurred them.

nation. The general truth of the matter is, that the Popes of the middle ages, like some other persons and professions, throve upon the discords of their neighbours. Other powers were only somewhere: the Pope, in the West, was everywhere. Of the two parties to a quarrel, it was worth the while of each to bid for the assistance of the Pope against his enemy; and he that bid the highest, not merely in dry acknowledgment of the Papal prerogatives, but also commonly in the solid tribute of Peter's pence, or patronages, or other tangible advantages, most commonly got the support of the Pope. This is a brief and rude outline; but it is history, and the other is fiction.

But does Dr. Newman stand better at this point? He only grants the deposing power in the shape in which the Pope asks it; and he says the Pope only asks it on the conditions of which one is "an united consent of various nations." * In the Speech of the Pope, however, which he cites, there is nothing corresponding to this account. The Pope says distinctly, "of this right the *Fountain* is (not the Infallibility, but) the Pontifical Authority." The people of the middle ages—what did they do? made him an arbitrator or judge? No: but recognised in him that which—what? he was? no: but—"he IS; the Supreme Judge of Christendom." The right was not created, but "assisted, as was DUE to it, by the public law and common consent of the nations." If this is not enough, I will complete the demonstration. An early report of the Speech † from the Roman newspapers winds up the statement by describing the Deposing Power as—

"A right which the Popes, *invited by the call of the nations*, had to exercise, when the general good demanded it."

---

* Dr. Newman, p. 37.
† 'Tablet,' Nov. 21, 1874, Letter of C. S. D.

But in the authorised and final report* given in the Collection of the Speeches of Pius IX., this passage is corrected, and runs thus:—

> "A right which the Popes *exercised in virtue of their authority* when the general good demanded it." †

Thus Bishop Clifford and Dr. Newman are entirely at issue with the Pope respecting the deposing power. Will they not have to reconsider what they are to say, and what they are to believe? That power, it must be borne in mind, appears to have one of the firmest possible Pontifical foundations, in the Bull *Unam Sanctam*, which is admitted on all hands to be a declaration *ex cathedrâ*.

But it is not to the more moderate views of the Bishop and Dr. Newman that we are to resort for information on the ruling fashions of Roman doctrine. Among the really orthodox defenders of Vaticanism, who have supplied the large majority of Reproofs and Replies, I do not recollect to have found one single disavowal of the deposing power. Perhaps the nearest approach to it from any writer of this school is supplied by Monsignor Capel, who remarks that the Pope's office of arbiter is at an end, or "at least *in* abeyance." ‡ There are, indeed, enough of disavowals wholly valueless. For example, disavowals of the universal monarchy; by which it appears to be meant that the Popes never claimed, in temporals, such a monarchical power as is now accorded to them in spirituals, namely a

---

* 'Discorsi di Pio IX.' vol. i. p. 203.

† 'Tablet' original (for which I am not responsible): "Un diritto, che i Papi, *chiamati dal voto dei popoli, dovettero esercitare* quando il comun bene lo domandava." Authorised original: "Un diritto che i Papi *esercitarono in virtù della loro Autorità*, quando il comun bene lo dimandava."

‡ Monsignor Capel, p. 60.

power absorbing and comprehending every other power whatever. Or again, disavowals of the *directa potestas*. For one, I attach not a feather's weight to the distinction between the direct power and the indirect. Speaking in his own person, Archbishop Manning eschews the gross assertions to which in another work he has lent a sanction,* and seems to think he has mended the position when he tells us that the Church, that is to say the Pope, "has a supreme judicial office, in respect to the moral law, over all nations, and over all persons, both governors and governed." As long as they do right, it is directive and preceptive; when they do wrong, the black cap of the judge is put on, *ratione peccati*, " by reason of sin." That is to say, in plain words, the right and the wrong in the conduct of States and of individuals is now, as it always has been, a matter for the judicial cognisance of the Church; and the entire judicial power of the Church is summed up in the Pope.

"If Christian princes and their laws deviate from the law of God, the Church has authority from God to judge of that deviation, and *by all its powers* to enforce the correction of that departure from justice."†

I must accord to the Archbishop the praise of manliness. If we are henceforward in any doubt as to his opinions, it is by our own fault. I sorrowfully believe, moreover, that he does no more than express the general opinion of the teachers who form the ruling body in his Church at large, and of the present Anglo-Romish clergy almost without exception. In the episcopal manifesto of Bishop Ullathorne I see nothing to qualify the doctrine. In the Pastoral Letter of Bishop Vaughan the comfort we obtain is this—"it will never, as we believe, be exercised again;" and "it is a question purely speculative. It is

---

* 'Essays,' edited by Archbishop Manning. London.
† Archbishop Manning, 'Vatican Decrees,' pp. 49-51.

no matter of Catholic faith, and is properly relegated to the schools."* Bishop Vaughan does not appear to bear in mind that this is exactly what we were told, not by his predecessors of 1789, who denied Infallibility outright: not by the Synod of 1810, who affirmed it to be impossible that Infallibility ever could become an article of faith; but even in the "bated breath" of later times with respect to Infallibility itself, which, a little while after, was called back from the schools and the speculative region, and uplifted into the list of the Christian *credenda*; and of which we are now told that it has been believed always, and by all, only its boundaries have been a little better marked.

In the train of the Bishops (I except Bishop Clifford) come priests, monks, nay, laymen: Vaticanism in all its ranks and orders. And among these champions, not one adopts the language even of Bishop Doyle, much less of 1810, much less of 1789. The "Monk of St. Augustine's" is not ashamed to say that Bishop Doyle, who was put forward in his day as the champion and representative man of the body, "held opinions openly at variance with those of the great mass."†

2. *Title to the use of Force.*

Equally clear, and equally unsatisfactory, are the Ultramontane declarations with respect to the title of the Church to employ force. Dr. Newman holds out a hand to brethren in distress by showing that a theological authority who inclines to the milder side, limits the kind of force, which the Church has of herself a right to employ.

---

* 'Pastoral Letter,' pp. 33, 34.
† See 'The Month,' Jan. 1875, pp. 82-4. Monk of St. Augustine's, p. 27, *seq*. Rev. J. Curry's 'Disquisition,' pp. 35, 41. Lord R. Montagu, 'Expostulation in extremis,' p. 51.

"The lighter punishments, though temporal and corporal, such as shutting up in a monastery, prison, flogging, and others of the same kind, short of effusion of blood, the Church, *jure suo,* can inflict."* And again: the Church does not claim the use of force generally, but only *that* use of force which Professor Nuytz denied.

We can from this source better understand the meaning of Archbishop Manning, when he states,† that the Church has authority from God to correct departures from justice by the use of "all its powers." The favourite mode of conveying this portion of truth—a portion so modest that it loves not to be seen—is by stating that the Church is a "perfect society." "The Church is a society complete and perfect in and by itself, and amply sufficing not only to bring men to salvation and everlasting bliss, but also to establish and perfectly regulate social life among them."‡ The Church has been created, says Bishop Vaughan, a "perfect society or kingdom," "with full authority in the triple order, as needful for a perfect kingdom, legislative, judicial, and coercive."§ His Metropolitan treats the subject at some length; assures us that the members of his communion would not make use of force even if they were able, but nowhere disclaims the right.‖ Indeed he cannot: he dares not. The inexorable Syllabus binds him to maintain it, as Ixion was bound to his wheel.

The subject, however, is one of the burning class; and it appears to terrify even Archbishop Manning. He refers us to the famous brief or letter of Innocent III., headed *Novit,* in his Appendix, where he states that the text is

---

* Cardinal Soglia, as cited by Dr. Newman, pp. 89, 90.
† 'Vatican Decrees,' p. 43.
‡ Martin, S.J., 'De Matrimonio, Notiones Præviæ,' ci.
§ 'Pastoral Letter,' p. 13.   ‖ See Appendix H.

given in full.* In the document, as it is there given, will be found the Pope's assertion, that it is his part to pass judgment on sovereigns in respect of sin (*ratione peccati*), and that he can coerce them by ecclesiastical constraint (*districtionem*). But the text of the brief is, according to my copy of the Decretals, not given in full; and the copyist has done the Pope scanty justice. He seems to have omitted what is the clearest and most important passage of the whole, since it distinctly shows that what is contemplated is the use of force.

"The Apostle also admonishes us to rebuke disturbers, and elsewhere he says: 'reprove, intreat, rebuke with all patience and doctrine.' Now that we are *able, and also bound to coerce*, is plain from this, that the Lord says to the Prophet, who was one of the priests of Anathoth: 'Behold, I have appointed thee over the nations and the kings, that thou mayest tear up, and pull down, and scatter, and build, and plant.'"†

With regard to Dr. Newman's limitation of the Proposition, I must cite an authority certainly higher in the Papal sense. The Jesuit Schrader has published, with a Papal approbation attached, a list of the affirmative propositions answering to the negative condemnations of the Syllabus. I extract his Article 24 :—‡

"The Church has the power to apply external coercion (*äusseren Zwang anzuwenden*): she has also a temporal authority direct and indirect."

The remark is appended, "Not souls alone are subject to her authority."

All, then, that I stated in the Expostulation, on the

* Archbishop Manning, p. 62 n.
† 'Corpus Juris Canonici Decret. Greg. IX.,' II. 1. 13. I cite from Richter's ed. (Leipsic, 1839). It has the pretensions, and I believe the character, of a critical and careful edition. I do not however presume to determine the textual question.
‡ Schrader, as above, p. 64.

Deposing Power, and on the claims of the Roman Church to employ force, is more than made good.

It was, I suppose, to put what Burnet would call a face of propriety on these and such like tenets, that one of the combatants opposed to me in the present controversy has revived an ingenious illustration of that clever and able writer, the late Cardinal Wiseman. He held that certain doctrines present to us an unseemly appearance, because we stand outside the Papal Church, even as the most beautiful window of stained glass in a church offers to those without only a confused congeries of paint and colours, while it is, to an eye viewing it from within, all glory and all beauty. But what does this amount to? It is simply to say, that when we look at the object in the free air and full light of day which God has given us, its structure is repulsive and its arrangement chaotic; but, if we will part with a great portion of that light, by passing within the walls of a building made by the hand of man, then, indeed, it will be better able to bear our scrutiny. It is an ill recommendation of a commodity, to point out that it looks the best where the light is scantiest.

VII. WARRANT OF ALLEGIANCE ACCORDING TO THE VATICAN.

1. *Its alleged Superiority.*
2. *Its real Flaws.*
3. *Alleged Non-interference of the Popes for Two Hundred Years.*

NOT satisfied with claiming to give guarantees for allegiance equal to those of their fellow-citizens, the champions of the Vatican have boldly taken a position in advance. They hold that they are in a condition to offer better warranty than ours, and this because they are guided by an infallible Pope, instead of an erratic private judgment; and because the Pope himself is exceedingly emphatic, even in the Syllabus, on the duties of subjects towards their rulers. Finally, all this is backed and riveted by an appeal to conduct. "The life and conduct of the Church for eighteen centuries are an ample guarantee for her love of peace and justice."* I would rather not discuss this " ample guarantee." Perhaps the Bishop's appeal might shake one who believed: I am certain it would not quiet one who doubted.

The inculcation of civil obedience under the sanction of religion is, so far as I am aware, the principle and practice of all Christian communities. We must therefore look a little farther into the matter in order to detect the distinctive character, in this respect, of the Vatican.

1. Unquestionably the Pope, and all Popes, are full and

---

* Bishop Vaughan, p. 28.

emphatic on the duties of subjects to rulers; but of what subjects to what rulers? It is the Church of England which has ever been the extravagantly loyal Church; I mean which has, in other days, exaggerated the doctrine of civil obedience, and made it an instrument of much political mischief. Passive obedience, non-resistance, and Divine right, with all of good or evil they involve, were specifically her ideas. In the theology now dominant in the Church of Rome, the theology which has so long had its nest in the Roman Court, these ideas prevail, but with a rider to them: obedience is to be given, Divine right is to belong, to those Princes and Governments which adopt the views of Rome, or which promote her interests: to those Princes and Governments which do right, Rome being the measure of right. I have no doubt that many outside the charmed circle praise in perfect good faith the superior bouquet and body of the wine of Roman Catholic loyalty. But those within, can they make such assertions? This is not easy to believe. The great art, nowhere else so well understood or so largely practised, is, in these matters, to seem to assert without asserting. This has been well-known at least for near five centuries, since the time of Gerson, whose name for Vaticanism is *Adulatio*. "*Sentiens autem Adulatio quandoque nimis se cognosci, studet quasi modiciore sermone depressiùs uti, ut credibilior appareat.*"* I must say that, if Vaticanists have on this occasion paraded the superior quality of the article they vend as loyalty, they have also supplied us with the means of testing the assertion; because one and all of them assert the corrective power of the Pope over Christian Sovereigns.

---

* 'De Potest. Eccl.,' Consideratio XII. Works, ii. 246, ed. Hague, 1728.

and Governments. I do not dispute that their commodity is good, in this country, for every-day tear and wear. But as to its ultimate groundwork and principle, on which in other places, and other circumstances, it might fall back, of this I will now cite a description from one of the very highest authorities; from an epistle of a most able and conspicuous Pontiff, to whom reference has already been made, I mean Nicholas the First.

When that Pontiff was prosecuting with iron will the cause against the divorce of Lothair from Theutberga, he was opposed by some Bishops within the dominions of the Emperor. Adventitius, Bishop of Metz, pleaded the duty of obeying his sovereign. Nicholas in reply described his view of that matter in a passage truly classical, which I translate from the Latin, as it is given in Baronius.

> "You allege, that you subject yourself to Kings and Princes, because the Apostle says 'Whether to the king, as in authority.' Well and good. Examine, however, whether the Kings and Princes, to whom you say that you submit, are truly Kings and Princes. Examine whether they govern well, first themselves, then the people under them. For if one be evil to himself, how shall he be good to others? Examine whether they conduct themselves rightly as Princes; for otherwise they are rather to be deemed tyrants, than taken for Kings, and we should resist them, and mount up against them, rather than be under them. Otherwise, if we submit to such, and do not put ourselves over them, we must of necessity encourage them in their vices. Therefore be subject 'to the King, as in authority, in his virtues that is to say, not his faults; as the Apostle says, for the sake of God, not against God.'"*

I cite the passage, not to pass a censure in the case, but for its straightforward exposition of the doctrine, now openly and widely preferred, though not so lucidly expounded, by the teaching body of the Romish Church.

---

* Baronius, A.D. 863, c. lxx.

Plainly enough, in point of right, the title of the temporal Sovereign is valid or null according to the view which may be taken by the Pope of the nature of his conduct. "No just prince," says Archbishop Manning, can be deposed by any power on earth; but whether a prince is just or not, is a matter for the Pope to judge of.*

We are told, indeed, that it is not now the custom for the Pope to depose princes: not even Victor Emmanuel.† True: he does no more than exhort the crowds who wait upon him in the Vatican to seek for the restoration of those Italian sovereigns whom the people have driven out. But no man is entitled to take credit for not doing that which he has no power to do. And one of the many irregularities in the mode of argument pursued by Vaticanism is, that such credit is constantly taken for not attempting the impossible. It is as if Louis XVI., when a prisoner in the Temple, had vaunted his own clemency in not putting the head of Robespierre under the guillotine.

But there are other kinds of interference and aggression, just as intolerable in principle as the exercise, or pretended exercise, of the deposing power. Have they been given up? We shall presently see.‡

2. *Its real Flaws.*

Cooks and controversialists seem to have this in common, that they nicely appreciate the standard of knowledge in those whose appetites they supply. The cook is tempted to send up ill-dressed dishes to masters who have slight skill in or care for cookery; and the

---

* Archbishop Manning, p. 46.
† Bishop Vaughan, 'Pastoral,' p. 34.
‡ *Infra*, p. 88.

controversialist occasionally shows his contempt for the intelligence of his readers by the quality of the arguments or statements which he presents for their acceptance. But this, if it is to be done with safety, should be done in measure; and I must protest that Vaticanism really went beyond all measure when it was bold enough to contend that its claims in respect to the civil power are the same as those which are made by the Christian communions generally of modern times. The sole difference, we are told, is that in one case the Pope, in the other the individual, determines the instances when obedience is to be refused; and as the Pope is much wiser than the individual, the difference in the Roman view is all in favour of the order of civil society.

The reader will, I hope, pay close attention to this portion of the subject. The whole argument greatly depends upon it. Before repealing the penal laws, before granting political equality, the statesmen of this country certainly took a very different view. They thought the Roman Catholic, as an individual citizen, was trustworthy. They were not afraid of relying even upon the local Church. What they were anxious to ascertain, and what, as far as men can through language learn the thought and heart of man, they did ascertain, was this; whether the Roman Catholic citizen, and whether the local Church, were free to act, or were subjected to an extraneous authority. This superior wisdom of the Pope of Rome was the very thing of which they had had ample experience in the middle ages; which our Princes and Parliaments long before the reign of Henry VIII. and the birth of Anna Boleyn, had wrought hard to control, and which the Bishops of the sixteenth century, including Tunstal and Stokesley, Gardiner and Bonner, used their best learning to exclude. Those who in 1875 propound the doctrine, which no single century of the middle ages would have admitted, must indeed have a mean opinion of any intellects which their language could cajole.

As a rule, the real independence of States and nations depends upon the exclusion of foreign influence proper from their civil affairs. Wherever the spirit of freedom, even if ever so faintly, breathes, it resents and reacts against any intrusion of another people or Power into the circle of its interior concerns, as alike dangerous and disgraceful. As water finds its level, so, in a certain tolerable manner, the various social forces of a country, if left to themselves, settle down into equilibrium. In the normal posture of things, the State ought to control, and can control, its subjects sufficiently for civil order and peace; and the normal is also the ordinary case, in this respect, through the various countries of the civilised world. But the essential condition of this ability, on which all depends, is that the forces, which the State is to govern, shall be forces having their seat within its own territorial limits. The power of the State is essentially a local power.

But the *Triregno* of the Pope, figured by the Tiara, touches heaven, earth, and Purgatory (*Discorsi*, i. 133). We now deal only with the earthly province. As against the local sway of the State, the power of the Pope is ubiquitous; and the whole of it can be applied at any point within the dominions of any State, although the far larger part of it does not arise within its borders, but constitutes, in the strictest sense, a foreign force. The very first condition of State-rule is thus vitally compromised.

The power, with which the State has thus to deal, is one dwelling beyond its limits, and yet beyond the reach of its arm. All the subjects of the State are responsible to the

State: they must obey, or they must take the consequences. But for the Pope there are no consequences: he is not responsible.

But it may be said, and it is true, that the State will not be much the better for the power it possesses of sending all its subjects to prison for disobedience. And here we come upon the next disagreeable distinction in the case of the Roman Church. She alone arrogates to herself the right to speak to the State, not as a subject but as a superior; not as pleading the right of a conscience staggered by the fear of sin, but as a vast Incorporation, setting up a rival law against the State in the State's own domain, and claiming for it, with a higher sanction, the title to similar coercive means of enforcement.

No doubt, mere submission to consequences is, for the State, an inadequate compensation for the mischief of disobedience. The State has duties which are essential to its existence, and which require active instruments. Passive resistance, widely enough extended, would become general anarchy. With the varying and uncombined influences of individual judgment and conscience, the State can safely take its chance. But here is a Power that claims authority to order the millions; and to rule the rulers of the millions, whenever, in its judgment, those rulers may do wrong.

The first distinction then is, that the Pope is himself foreign and not responsible to the law; the second, that the larger part of his power is derived from foreign sources; the third, that he claims to act, and acts, not by individuals, but on masses; the fourth, that he claims to teach them, so often as he pleases, what to do at each point of their contact with the laws of their country.

Even all this might be borne, and might be comparatively harmless but for that at which I have already glanced. He alone of all ecclesiastical powers presumes not only to limit the domain of the State, but to meet the State in its own domain. The Presbyterian Church of Scotland showed a resolution never exceeded, before the secession of 1843, in resisting the civil power; but it offered the resistance of submission. It spoke for the body, and its ministers in things concerning it: but did not presume to command the private conscience. Its modest language would be far from filling the *os rotundum* of a Roman Pontiff. Nay, the words of the Apostle do not suffice for him. St. Peter himself was not nearly so great as his Successor. He was content with the modest excuse of the individual: "We ought to obey God rather than man."[*] Rome has improved upon St. Peter: 'Your laws and ordinances we proscribe and condemn, and declare them to be absolutely, both hereafter and from the first, null, void, and of no effect.' That is to say, the Pope takes into his own hand the power which he thinks the State to have misused. Not merely does he aid or direct the conscience of those who object, but he even overrules the conscience of those who approve. Above all, he pretends to annul the law itself.

Such is the fifth point of essential distinction between these monstrous claims, and the modest though in their proper place invincible exigencies of the private conscience. But one void still remains unfilled; one plea not yet unmasked. Shall it be said, this is all true, but it is all spiritual, and therefore harmless? An idle answer at the best, for the origin of spiritual power is and ought to be a real one, and ought not therefore to be used against the civil order: but worse than idle, because

---

[*] Acts v. 29.

totally untrue, inasmuch as we are now told in the plainest terms (negatively in the Syllabus, affirmatively in Schrader's approved conversion of it),* that the Church is invested with a temporal power direct and indirect, and has authority to employ external coercion.

Am I not right in saying, that after all this to teach the identity of the claims of Vaticanism with those of other forms of Christianity in the great and grave case of conscience against the civil power, is simply to manifest a too thinly veiled contempt for the understanding of the British community, for whose palate and digestion such diet has been offered?

The exact state of the case, as I believe, is this. The right to override all the States of the world and to cancel their acts, within limits assignable from time to time to, but not by those States, and the title to do battle with them, as soon as it may be practicable and expedient, with their own proper weapon and last sanction of exterior force, has been sedulously brought more and more into view of late years. The centre of the operation has lain in the Society of Jesuits; I am loath to call them by the sacred name, which ought never to be placed in the painful associations of controversy. In 1870, the fulness of time was come. The *matter* of the things to be believed and obeyed had been sufficiently developed. But inasmuch as great masses of the Roman Catholic body before that time refused either to believe or to obey, in that year the bold stroke was struck, and it was decided to bring mischievous abstractions if possible into the order of still more mischievous realities. The infallible, that is virtually the Divine, title to command, and the absolute, that is the

---

* Schrader, as above, p. 64.

unconditional duty to obey, were promulgated to an astonished world.

3. *Alleged non-interference of the Popes for Two Hundred Years.*

It has been alleged on this occasion by a British Peer, who I have no doubt has been cruelly misinformed, that the Popes have not invaded the province of the civil power during the last two hundred years. I will not travel over so long a period, but am content even with the last twenty.

1. In his Allocution of the 22nd January, 1855, Pius IX. declared to be absolutely null and void all acts of the Government of Piedmont which he held to be in prejudice of the rights of Religion, the Church, and the Roman See, and particularly a law proposed for the suppression of the monastic orders as moral entities, that is to say as civil corporations.

2. On the 26th of July in the same year, Pius IX. sent forth another Allocution, in which he recited various acts of the Government of Spain, including the establishment of toleration for non-Roman worship, and the secularisation of ecclesiastical property; and, by his own apostolical authority, he declared all the laws hereto relating to be abrogated, totally null, and of no effect.

3. On the 22nd of June, 1862, in another Allocution, Pius IX. recited the provisions of an Austrian law of the previous December, which established freedom of opinion, of the press, of belief, of conscience, of science, of education, and of religious profession, and which regulated matrimonial jurisdiction and other matters. The whole of these "abominable" laws "have been and shall be totally void, and without all force whatsoever."

In all these cases reference is made, in general terms, to Concordats, of which the Pope alleges the violation; but he never bases his annulment of the laws upon this allegation. And Schrader, in his work on the Syllabus, founds the cancellation of the Spanish law, in the matter of toleration, not on the Concordat, but on the original inherent right of the Pope to enforce the 77th Article of the Syllabus, respecting the exclusive establishment of the Roman religion.*

To provide, however, against all attempts to take refuge in this specialty, I will now give instances where no question of Concordat enters at all into the case.

1. In an Allocution of July 27, 1855, when the law for the suppression of monastic orders and appropriation of their properties had been passed in the kingdom of Sardinia, on the simple ground of his Apostolic authority, the Pope annuls this law, and all other laws injurious to the Church, and excommunicates all who had a hand in them.

2. In an Allocution of December 15, 1856, the Pope recites the interruption of negotiations for a Concordat with Mexico, and the various acts of that Government against religion, such as the abolition of the ecclesiastical *forum*, the secularisation of Church property, and the civil permission to members of monastic establishments to withdraw from them. All of these laws are declared absolutely null and void.

3. On the 17th of September, 1863, in an Encyclical Letter the Pope enumerates like proceedings on the part of the Government of New Granada. Among the wrongs committed, we find the establishment of freedom of worship (*cujusque acatholici cultûs libertas sancita*). These and all

---

* Schrader, p. 80.

other acts against the Church, utterly unjust and impious, the Pope, by his Apostolic authority, declares to be wholly null and void in the future and in the past.*

No more, I hope, will be heard of the allegation that for two hundred years the Popes have not attempted to interfere with the Civil Powers of the world.

But if it be requisite to carry proof a step farther, this may readily be done. In his ' Petri Privilegium,' iii. 19, n., Archbishop Manning quotes the Bull *In Cœnâ Domini* as if it were still in force. Bishop Clifford, in his Pastoral Letter (p. 9), laid it down that though all human actions were moral actions, there were many of them which belonged to the temporal power, and with which the Pope could not interfere. Among these he mentioned the assessment and payment of taxes. But is it not the fact that this Bull excommunicates "all who impose new taxes, not already provided for by law, without the Pope's leave?" and all who impose, without the said leave, special and express, any taxes, new or old, upon clergymen, churches, or monasteries? †

I may be told that Archbishop Manning is not a safe authority in these matters, that the Bull *In Cœnâ Domini* was withdrawn after the assembling of the Council, and the constitution *Apostolicæ Sedis* ‡ substituted for it, in

---

* All these citations, down to 1865, will be found in 'Recueil des Allocutions Consistoriales,' &c. (Paris, 1865, Adrien Leclero et Cie). See also ' Europäische Geschichtskalender,' 1868, p. 249 ; Von Schulte, ' Powers of the Roman Popes,' iv. 43 ; Schrader, as above, Heft ii. p. 80 ; ' Vering, 'Katholisches Kirchenrecht' (Mainz, 1868), Band xx. pp. 170, 1, N. F. Band xiv.

† O'Keeffe, 'Ultramontanism,' pp. 215, 219. The reference is to sections v., xviii.

‡ See Quirinus, p. 105 ; and see ' Constit. Apostolicæ Sedis ' in Friedberg's ' Acta et Decreta Conc. Vat.,' p. 77 (Friburg, 1871).

which this reference to taxes is omitted. But if this be so, is it not an astonishing fact, with reference to the spirit of Curialism, that down to the year 1870 these preposterous claims of aggression should have been upheld and from time to time proclaimed? Indeed the new Constitution itself, dated October, 1869, the latest specimen of reform and concession, without making any reservation whatever on behalf of the laws of the several countries, excommunicates (among others)—

1. All who imprison or prosecute (*hostiliter insequentes*) Archbishops or Bishops.

2. All who directly or indirectly interfere with any ecclesiastical jurisdiction.

3. All who lay hold upon or sequester goods of ecclesiastics held in right of their churches or benefices.

4. All who impede or deter the officers of the Holy Office of the Inquisition in the execution of their duties.

5. All who secularise, or become owners of, Church property, without the permission of the Pope.

VIII. ON THE INTRINSIC NATURE AND CONDITIONS OF THE PAPAL INFALLIBILITY DECREED IN THE VATICAN COUNCIL.

I HAVE now, I think, dealt sufficiently, though at greater length than I could have wished, with the two allegations, first, that the Decrees of 1870 made no difference in the liabilities of Roman Catholics with regard to their civil allegiance; secondly, that the rules of their Church allow them to pay an allegiance no more divided than that of other citizens, and that the claims of Ultramontanism, as against the Civil Power, are the very same with those which are advanced by Christian communions and persons generally.

I had an unfeigned anxiety to avoid all discussion of the Decree of Infallibility on its own, the religious, ground; but as matters have gone so far, it may perhaps be allowed me now to say a few words upon the nature of the extraordinary tenet, which the Bishops of one half the Christian world have now placed upon a level with the Apostles' Creed.

The name of Popery, which was formerly imposed *ad invidiam* by heated antagonists, and justly resented by Roman Catholics,* appears now to be perhaps the only name which describes, at once with point and with accuracy, the religion promulgated from the Vatican in 1870. The change made was immense. Bishop Thirlwall, one of the ablest English writers of our time, and one imbued almost beyond any other with what the Germans eulogise as the historic mind, said in his Charge of 1872, that the

---

* 'Petri Privilegium,' part ii. pp. 71–91.

promulgation of the new Dogma, which had occurred since his last meeting with his clergy, was "an event far more important than the great change in the balance of power, which we have witnessed during the same interval."*
The effect of it, described with literal rigour, was in the last resort to place the entire Christian religion in the breast of the Pope, and to suspend it on his will. This is a startling statement; but as it invites, so will it bear, examination. I put it forth not as rhetoric, sarcasm, or invective; but as fact, made good by history.

It is obvious to reply that, if the Christian religion is in the heart of the Pope, so the law of England is in the heart of the Legislature. The case of the Pope and the case of the Legislature are the same in this: that neither the one nor the other is subject to any limitation whatever, except such as he or it respectively shall choose to allow. Here the resemblance begins and ends. The nation is ruled by a Legislature, of which by far the most powerful branch is freely chosen, from time to time, by the community itself by the greater part of the heads of families in the country; and all the proceedings of its Parliament are not only carried on in the face of day, but made known from day to day, almost from hour to hour, in every town and village, and almost in every household of the land. They are governed by rules framed to secure both ample time for consideration, and the utmost freedom, or, it may be, even licence of debate; and all that is said and done is subjected to an immediate sharp and incessant criticism: with the assurance on the part of the critics, that they will have not only favour from their friends, but impunity from their enemies. Erase every one of these propositions,

---

* 'Charge of the Bishop of St. David's,' 1872, p. 2.

and replace it by its contradictory; you will then have a perfect description of the present Government of the Roman Church. The ancient principles of popular election and control, for which room was found in the Apostolic Church under its inspired teachers, and which still subsist in the Christian East, have, by the constant aggressions of Curialism, been in the main effaced, or, where not effaced, reduced to the last stage of practical inanition. We see before us the Pope, the Bishops, the priesthood, and the people. The priests are absolute over the people; the Bishops over both; the Pope over all. Each inferior may appeal against his superior; but he appeals to a tribunal which is secret, which is irresponsible, which he has no share, direct or indirect, in constituting, and no means, however remote, of controlling; and which, during all the long centuries of its existence, but especially during the latest of them, has had for its cardinal rule this—that all its judgments should be given in the sense most calculated to build up priestly power as against the people, episcopal power as against the priests, Papal power as against all three. The mere utterances of the central See are laws; and they override at will all other laws: and if they concern faith or morals, or the discipline of the Church, they are entitled, from all persons without exception, singly or collectively, to an obedience without qualification. Over these utterances—in their preparation as well as after their issue—no man has lawful control. They may be the best, or the worst; the most deliberate, or the most precipitate: as no man can restrain, so no man has knowledge of, what is done or meditated. The prompters are unknown; the consultees are unknown; the procedure is unknown. Not that there are not officers, and rules; but the officers may at will be overridden or superseded;

and the rules at will, and without notice, altered *pro re natâ* and annulled. To secure rights has been, and is, the aim of the Christian civilisation : to destroy them, and to establish the resistless, domineering action of a purely central power, is the aim of the Roman policy. Too much and too long, in other times, was this its tendency : but what was its besetting sin has now become, as far as man can make it, by the crowning triumph of 1870, its undisguised, unchecked rule of action and law of life.

These words, harsh as they may seem, and strange as they must sound, are not the incoherent imaginings of adverse partisanship. The best and greatest of the children of the Roman Church have seen occasion to use the like, with cause less grave than that which now exists, and have pointed to the lust of dominion as the source of these enormous mischiefs :—

> "Dì oggimai, che la Chiesa di Roma
> Per confondere in se due reggimenti
> Cade nel fango, e se brutta, e la soma."*

Without doubt there is an answer to all this. Publicity, responsibility, restraint, and all the forms of warranty and safeguard, are wanted for a human institution, but are inapplicable to a "Divine teacher," to an inspired Pontiff, to a "living Christ." The promises of God are sure, and fail not. His promise has been given, and Peter in his Successor shall never fail, never go astray. He needs neither check nor aid, as he will find them for himself. He is an exception to all the rules which determine human action ; and his action in this matter is not really human,

---

* Dante, 'Purgatorio,' xvi. 127—9.
> "The Church of Rome,
> Mixing two governments that ill assort,
> Hath missed her footing, fallen into the mire,
> And there herself, and burden, much defiled."—*Cary.*

but Divine. Having, then, the Divine gift of inerrancy, why may he not be invested with the title, and assume the Divine attribute, of omnipotence?

No one can deny that the answer is sufficient, if only it be true. But the weight of such a superstructure requires a firm, broad, well-ascertained foundation. If it can be shown to exist, so far so good. In the due use of the gift of reason with which our nature is endowed, we may look for a blessing from God; but the abandonment of reason is credulity, and the habit of credulity is presumption.

Is there, then, such a foundation disclosed to us by Dr. Newman* when he says "the long history of the contest for and against the Pope's infallibility has been but a growing insight through centuries into the meaning of three texts"? First, "Feed my sheep" (John xxi. 15-17); of which Archbishop Kenrick tells us that the very words are disputed, and the meaning forced.† Next, "Strengthen thy brethren;" which has no reference whatever to doctrine, but only, if its force extend beyond the immediate occasion, to government; and, finally, "Thou art Peter, and on this rock I will build my Church;" when it is notorious that the large majority of the early expositors declare the rock to be not the person but the previous confession of Saint Peter; and where it is plain that, if his person be really meant, there is no distinction of *ex Cathedrâ* and not *ex Cathedrâ*, but the entire proceedings of his ministry are included without distinction.

---

* Dr. Newman, p. 110.

† 'Concio habenda at non habita,' i. ii. Friedrich, 'Documenta ad illustrandum,' Conc. Vat. Abth. i. pp. 191, 199. I leave it to those better entitled and better qualified to criticise the purely arbitrary construction attached to the words. Upon inquiry, I find the MSS. give serious grounds of doubt as to the received text.

Into three texts, then, it seems the Church of Rome has at length, in the course of centuries, acquired this deep insight. In the study of these three fragments, how much else has she forgotten! the total ignorance of St. Peter himself respecting his "monarchy;" the exercise of the defining office not by him but by St. James in the Council of Jerusalem; the world-wide commission specially and directly given to St. Paul; the correction of St. Peter by the Apostle of the Gentiles; the independent action of all the Apostles; the twelve foundations of the New Jerusalem, "and in them the names of the twelve Apostles of the Lamb" (Rev. xxi. 14). But let us take a wider ground. Is it not the function of the Church to study the Divine Word as a whole, and to gather into the foci of her teaching the rays that proceed from all its parts? Is not this narrow, sterile, wilful, textualism the favourite resort of sectaries, the general charter of all licence and self-will that lays waste the garden of the Lord? Is it not this that destroys the largeness and fair proportions of the Truth, squeezing here and stretching there, substituting for the reverent jealousy of a faithful guardianship the ambitious aims of a class, and gradually forcing the heavenly pattern into harder and still harder forms of distortion and caricature?

However, it must be observed that the transcendental answer we have been considering, which sets at nought all the analogies of God's Providence in the government of the world, is the only answer of a breadth equal to the case. Other replies, which have been attempted, are perfectly hollow and unreal. For instance, we are told that the Pope cannot alter the already defined doctrines of the Faith. To this I reply, let him alter them as he will, if only he thinks fit to say that he does not alter

H

them, his followers are perfectly and absolutely helpless. For if they allege alteration and innovation, the very same language will be available against them which has been used against the men that have had faith and courage given them to protest against alteration and innovation now. "Most impious are you, in charging on us that which, as you know, we cannot do. We have not altered, we have only defined. What the Church believed implicitly heretofore, she believes implicitly hereafter. Do not appeal to reason; that is rationalism. Do not appeal to Scripture; that is heresy. Do not appeal to history; that is private judgment. Over all these things I am judge, not you. If you tell me that I require you to affirm to-day, under anathema, what yesterday you were allowed or encouraged to deny, my answer is that in and by me alone you have any means of knowing what it is you affirm, or what it is you deny." This is the strain which is consistently held by the bold trumpeters of Vaticanism, and which has been effectual to intimidate the feeble-minded and faint-hearted, who seem to have formed, at the Council of the Vatican, so large a proportion of its opponents; nay, which has convinced them, or has performed in them the inscrutable process, be it what it may, which is the Roman substitute for conviction, that what in the Council itself they denounced as breach of faith, after the Council they are permitted, nay bound, to embrace, nay to enforce.

Let me now refer to another of these fantastic replies.

We are told it would be an entire mistake to confound this Infallibility of the Pope, in the province assigned to it, with absolutism:—

"The Pope is bound by the moral and divine law, by the commandments of God, by the rules of the Gospel, and by every definition in faith and morals that the Church has ever made. No man is more bound by law than the Pope; a fact plainly known to himself, and to every bishop and priest in Christendom."*

Every definition in faith and morals! These are written definitions. What are they but another Scripture? What right of interpreting this other Scripture is granted to the Church at large, more than of the real and greater Scripture? Here is surely, in its perfection, the petition for bread, answered by the gift of a stone.

Bishop Vaughan does not venture to assert that the Pope is bound by the canon law, the written law of the Church of Rome. The abolition of the French Sees under the Concordat with Napoleon, and the deposition of their legitimate Bishops, even if it were the only instance, has settled that question for ever. Over the written law of his Church the pleasure of the Pope is supreme. And this justifies, for every practical purpose, the assertion that law no longer exists in that Church; in the same very real sense as we should say there was no law in England in the reign of James the Second, while it was subject to a dispensing power. There exists no law, wherever a living ruler, an executive head, claims and exercises, and is allowed to possess, a power of annulling or a power of dispensing with the law. If Bishop Vaughan does not know this, I am sorry to say he does not know the first lesson that every English citizen should learn; he has yet to pass through the lispings of civil childhood. This exemption of the individual, be he who he may, from the restraints of the law is the very thing that in England we term absolutism. By absolutism we mean the superiority of a personal will to law, for the purpose of putting aside or changing law. Now that power is precisely what

---

* Bishop Vaughan's 'Pastoral Letter,' p. 30.

the Pope possesses. First, because he is infallible in faith and morals, when he speaks *ex cathedrâ*, and he himself is the final judge which of his utterances shall be utterances *ex cathedrâ*. He has only to use the words, " I, *ex cathedrâ*, declare ;" or the words, " I, in the discharge of the office of pastor and teacher of all Christians, by virtue of my supreme Apostolic authority, define as a doctrine regarding faith or morals, to be held by the Universal Church ;"* and all words that may follow, be they what they may, must now and hereafter be as absolutely accepted by every Roman Catholic who takes the Vatican for his teacher, with what in their theological language they call a Divine faith, as must any article of the Apostles' Creed. And what words they are to be that may follow, the Pope by his own will and motion is the sole judge.

It is futile to say, the Pope has the Jesuits and other admirable advisers near him, whom he will always consult. I am bound to add that I am sceptical as to the excellence of these advisers. These are the men who cherish, methodise, transmit, and exaggerate, all the dangerous traditions of the Curia. In them it lives. The ambition and self-seeking of the Court of Rome have here their root. They seem to supply that Roman *malaria*, which Dr. Newman† tells us encircles the base of the rock of St. Peter. But the question is not what the Pope will do ; it is what he can do, what he has power to do ; whether, in Bishop Vaughan's language, he is bound by law ; not whether he is so wise and so well-advised that it is perfectly safe to leave him not bound by law. On this latter question there may be a great conflict of opinions ; but it is not the question before us.

---

* 'Vatican Decrees,' chap. iii.
† Dr. Newman, p. 94.

ON THE NATURE OF THE PAPAL INFALLIBILITY. 101

It cannot be pleaded against him, were it ever so clear, that his declaration is contrary to the declaration of some other Popes. For here, as in the case of the Christian Creed, he may tell you—always speaking in the manner supposed—that that other Pope was not speaking *ex cathedrâ*. Or he may tell you that there is no contrariety. If you have read, if you have studied, if you have seen, if you have humbly used every means of getting to the truth, and you return to your point that *contrariety there is*, again his answer is ready: That assertion of yours is simply your private judgment; and your private judgment is just what my infallibility is meant and appointed to put down. My word is the tradition of the Church. It is the nod of Zeus: it is the judgment of the Eternal. There is no escaping it, and no disguising it: the whole Christian religion, according to the modern Church of Rome, is in the breast of one man. The will and arbitrament of one man will for the future decide, through half the Christian world, what religion is to be. It is unnecessary to remind me that this power is limited to faith and morals. We know it is; it does not extend to geometry, or to numbers. Equally is it beside the point to observe that the infallibility alleged has not received a new definition: I have nowhere said it had. It is the old gift: it is newly lodged. Whatever was formerly ascribed either to the Pope, or to the Council, or to the entire governing body of the Church, or to the Church general and diffused, the final sense of the great Christian community, aided by authority, tested by discussion, mellowed and ripened by time—all—no more than all, and no less than all—of what God gave, for guidance, through the power of truth, by the Christian revelation, to the whole redeemed family, the baptized flock of the Saviour in the world; all this is now locked in the breast of one man, opened and distributed at his will, and liable to assume whatever form—whether under the name of identity or other name it matters not—he may think fit to give it.

Idle then it is to tell us, finally, that the Pope is bound "by the moral and divine law, by the commandments of God, by the rules of the Gospel:" and if more verbiage and repetition could be piled up, as Ossa was set upon Olympus, and Pelion upon Ossa, to cover the poverty and irrelevancy of the idea, it would not mend the matter. For of these, one and all, the Pope himself, by himself, is the judge without appeal. If he consults, it is by his will: if he does not consult, no man can call him to account. No man, or assemblage of men, is one whit the less bound to hear and to obey. He is the judge of the moral and Divine law, of the Gospel, and of the commandments; the supreme and only final judge: and he is the judge, with no legislature to correct his errors, with no authoritative rules to guide his proceedings: with no power on earth to question the force, or intercept the effect, of his decisions.

It is indeed said by Dr. Newman, and by others, that this infallibility is not inspiration. On such a statement I have two remarks to make. First, that we have this assurance on the strength only of his own private judgment; secondly, that if bidden by the self-assertion of the Pope, he will be required by his principles to retract it,[*] and to assert, if occasion should arise, the contrary; thirdly, that he lives under a system of development, through which somebody's private opinion of to-day may become matter of faith for all the to-morrows of the future. What kind and class of private opinions are they that are

---

[*] Dr. Newman, pp. 99, 131. The Papal newspaper, 'Voce della Verità,' of Jan. 21 complains seriously of parts of Dr. Newman's Reply.

most likely to find favour with the Vatican? History, the history of well-nigh eighteen centuries, supplies the answer, and supplies it with almost the rigour of a mathematical formula. On every contested question, that opinion finds ultimate assent at Rome, which more exalts the power of Rome. Have no Popes claimed this inspiration, which Dr. Newman so reasonably denies? Was it claimed by Clement XI. for the Bull *Unigenitus*? Was it claimed by Gregory the Second in a judgment in which he authorised a man, who had an invalid wife, to quit her and to marry another? Is it or is it not claimed by the present Pope, who says he has a higher title to admonish the governments of Europe than the Prophet Nathan had to admonish David?* Shall we be told that these are his utterances only as a private Doctor? But we also learn from Papal divines, and indeed the nature of the case makes it evident, that the non-infallible declarations of the Pope are still declarations of very high authority. Again, is it not the fact that, since 1870, many bishops, German, Italian, French, have ascribed inspiration to the Pope? Opinions dispersed here and there were, in the cases of the Immaculate Conception, and of the Absolute Supremacy and the Infallibility *ex cathedrâ*, gathered up, declared to constitute a *consensus* of the Church, and made the groundwork of new Articles of Faith. Why should not this be done hereafter in the case of Papal inspiration? It is but a mild onward step, in comparison with the strides already made. Those who cried "magnificent," on the last occasion, will cry it again on the next. Dr. Newman and the minimising divines would, perhaps, reply "No: it is impossible." But this was the very

---

* 'Discorsi di Pio IX.,' vol. i. p. 366, on March 3, 1872.

assurance which, not a single and half-recognised divine, but the whole synod of Irish prelates gave to the British Government in 1810, and which the Council of the Vatican has authoritatively falsified.

Now, let us look a little more closely at this astonishing gift of Infallibility, and its almost equally astonishing, because arbitrary, limitations. The Pope is only infallible when he speaks *ex cathedrâ*. The gift, we are told, has subsisted for 1800 years. When was the discriminating phrase invented? Was it after Christendom had done without it for one thousand six hundred years, that this limiting formula of such vital moment was discovered? Do we owe its currency and prominence—with so much else of ill omen—to the Jesuits? Before this, if we had not the name, had we the thing?

Dr. Newman, indeed, finds for it a very ancient extraction. He says the Jewish doctors taught *ex cathedrâ*, and our Saviour enjoined that they should be obeyed. Surely there could not be a more calamitous illustration. Observe the terms of the incoherent proposition.

The Scribes and Pharisees sit in the *cathedra* of Moses: "*all* therefore whatsoever they bid you observe, that observe and do."* The Pope sits in the *cathedra* of Peter, not all therefore, but only a very limited part of what he enjoins, you are to accept and follow. Only what he says under four well-defined conditions.† Only, writes Dr. Newman, when he speaks " in matters speculative,"‡ and " bears upon the domain of thought, not directly of action."‡ Let us look again to our four conditions: one of them is that he must address the entire Church. It is singular, to say no more, that St. Peter, in his first

---

* St. Matt. xxiii. 2.   † Newman, p. 115.   ‡ *Ibid.* p. 127.

Epistle, which has always been unquestioned Scripture, does not address the entire Church; but in his Second, which was for a time much questioned, he does. It is much more singular that the early ages are believed to afford no example whatever of a Papal judgment addressed to the entire Church. So that it is easy to say that Honorius did not speak *ex cathedrâ*: for no Pope spoke *ex cathedrâ*. It is even held by some that there was no Bull or other declaration of a Pope corresponding with this condition for one thousand three hundred years; and that the unhappy series began with *Unam Sanctam* of Boniface VIII. But how is it beyond all expression strange that for one thousand three hundred years, or were it but for half one thousand three hundred years, the Church performed her high office, and spread over the nations, without any infallible teaching whatever from the Pope, and then that it should have been reserved for these later ages first to bring into exercise a gift so entirely new, without example in its character, and on the presence or absence of which depends a vital difference in the conditions of Church life?

The declarations of the Pope *ex cathedrâ* are to be the sure guide and mainstay of the Church; and yet she has passed through two-thirds of her existence without once reverting to it! Nor is this all. For in those earlier ages, the fourth century in particular, were raised and settled those tremendous controversies relating to the Godhead, the decision of which was the most arduous work the Church has ever been called to perform in the sphere of thought. This vast work she went through without the infallible utterances of the Pope, nay at three several times in opposition to Papal judgments, now determined to have been heretical. Are more utterances now begun in order to sustain the miserable argument for forcing his

Temporal Sovereignty on a people, whom nothing but the violence of foreign arms will bring or keep beneath it?

Yet one more point of suggestion. There are those who think that the craving after an infallibility which is to speak from human lips, in chapter and verse, upon each question as it arises, is not a sign of the strength and healthiness of faith, but of the diseased avidity of its weakness. Let it, however, be granted, for the sake of argument, that it is a comfort to the infirmity of human nature thus to attain promptly to clear and intelligible solutions of its doubts, instead of waiting on the Divine pleasure, as those who watch for the morning, to receive the supplies required by its intellectual and its moral trials. A recommendation of this kind, however little it may endure the scrutiny of philosophic reflection, may probably have a great power over the imagination and the affections (*affectus*) of mankind. For this, however, it is surely required that by the ordinary faculties of mankind, rationally and honestly used, these infallible decisions should be discernible, and that they should stand severed from the general mass of promiscuous and ambiguous teaching. Even so it was that, when Holy Scripture was appointed to be of final and supreme authority, provision was also made by the wisdom of Providence for the early collection of the New Testament into a single series of Books, so that even we lay persons are allowed to know so far what is Scripture and what is not, without having to resort to the aid of the "scrutinising vigilance, acuteness, and subtlety of the *Schola Theologorum*."* But let not the Papal Christian imagine that he is to have a like advantage in easily understanding

---

* Dr. Newman, p. 121.

what are the Papal Decrees, which for him form part of the unerring revelation of God. It would even be presumptuous in him to have an opinion on the point. The Divine word of Scripture was invested with a power to feed and to refresh. " He shall feed me in a green pasture ; and lead me forth beside the waters of comfort."* And, by the blessing and mercy of God, straight and open is the access to them. In no part of the Church of Christ, except the Roman, is it jealously obstructed by ecclesiastical authority ; and even there the line of the sacred precinct is at least perfectly defined. But now we are introduced to a new code, dealing with the same high subject-matter, and possessed of the same transcendent prerogative of certain and unchanging truth ; but what are the chapters of that code, nobody knows except the *Schola Theologorum.* Is for example the private Christian less humbly desirous to know whether he is or is not to rely absolutely on the declarations of the Syllabus as to the many and great matters which it touches ? No one can tell him. Bishop Fessler (approved by the Pope) says so. He admits that he for one does not know. It seems doubtful whether he thought that the Pope himself knew. For instead of asking the Pope, he promises that it shall be made the subject of long inquiry by the *Schola Theologorum.* " *Ce sera tout d'abord à la science théologique que s'imposera le devoir de rechercher les diverses raisons qui militent en faveur des diverses opinions sur cette question.*" † But when the inquiry has ended, and the result has been declared, is he much better off ? I doubt

---

* Psalm xxiii. 2.
† 'Vraie et fausse Infaillibilité des Papes,' p. 8. Angl. : " It will at once become the duty of theological science to examine into the various reasons which go to support each of the various opinions on that question."

it. For the declaration need not then be a final one. "Instances," says Dr. Newman, "frequently occur, when it is successfully maintained by some new writer, that the Pope's act does not imply what it has seemed to imply; and questions, which seemed to be closed, are after a course of years reopened."* It does not appear whether there is any limit to this "course of years." But whether there is or is not, one thing is clear : Between the solid ground, the *terra firma* of Infallibility, and the quaking, fluctuating mind of the individual, which seeks to find repose upon it, there is an interval over which he cannot cross. Decrees *ex cathedrâ* are infallible; but determinations what decrees are *ex cathedrâ* are fallible; so that the private person, after he has with all docility handed over his mind and its freedom to the *Schola Theologorum*, can never certainly know, never know with "divine faith," when he is on the rock of infallibility, when on the shifting quicksands of a merely human persuasion.

Dr. Newman† will perhaps now be able to judge the reason which led me to say, "There is no established or accepted definition of the phrase *ex cathedrâ*." By a definition I understand something calculated to bring the true nature of the thing defined nearer to the rational apprehension of those who seek to understand it; not a volume of words in themselves obscure, only pliable to the professional interest of Curialism, and certainly well calculated to find further employment for its leisure, and fresh means of holding in dependence on its will an unsuspecting laity.

But all that has been said is but a slight sample of the strange aspects and portentous results of the newly discovered *articulus stantis aut cadentis ecclesiæ.*

CONCLUSION.

I HAVE now, at greater length than I could have wished, but I think with ample proof, justified the following assertions:—

1. That the position of Roman Catholics has been altered by the Decrees of the Vatican on Papal Infallibility, and on obedience to the Pope.

2. That the extreme claims of the Middle Ages have been sanctioned, and have been revived without the warrant or excuse which might in those ages have been shown for them.

3. That the claims asserted by the Pope are such as to place civil allegiance at his mercy.

4. That the State and people of the United Kingdom had a right to rely on the assurances they had received, that Papal Infallibility was not, and could not become, an article of faith in the Roman Church, and that the obedience due to the Pope was limited by laws independent of his will.

I need not any more refer to others of my assertions, more general, or less essential to the main argument.

The appeal of the 'Dublin Review'* for union on the basis of common belief in resisting unbelief, which ought to be strong, is unhappily very weak. "Defend," says the Reviewer, "the ark of salvation precious to us both, though you have an interest (so to speak) in only a part of the cargo." But as the Reviewer himself is deck-loading the vessel in such a manner as to threaten her foundering, to stop his very active proceedings is not

---

* For Jan. 1875, p. 173.

opposed to, nay, is part of, the duty of caring for the safety of the vessel. But weaker still, if possible, is the appeal which Archbishop Manning has made against my publication, as one which endeavours to create religious divisions among his flock, and instigate them to rise against the authority of the Church. For if the Church of England, of which I am a member, is, as she has never ceased to teach, the ancient, lawful, Catholic Church of this country, it is rather Archbishop Manning than I that may be charged with creating, for the last twenty years and more, religious divisions among our countrymen, and instigating them to rise against that ancient, lawful, and mild authority.

There may be, and probably are, great faults in my manner of conducting this argument. But the claim of Ultramontanism among us seems to amount to this : that there shall be no free, and therefore no effectual, examination of the Vatican Decrees, because they are the words of a Father, and sacred therefore in the eyes of his affectionate children.* It is deliberately held, by grave and serious men, that my construing the Decrees of the Vatican, not arbitrarily, but with argument and proof, in a manner which makes them adverse to civil duty, is an "insult" and an outrage to the Roman Catholic body, which I have nowhere charged with accepting them in that sense. Yet a far greater licence has been assumed by Archbishop Manning, who, without any attempt or proof at all, suggests,† if he does not assert, that the allegiance of the masses of the English people is an inert conformity and a passive compliance, given really for wrath and not for conscience' sake. This opinion is, in my judg-

---

* 'Dublin Review,' Jan. 1875, p. 172.
† Archbishop Manning, pp. 345.

ment, most untrue, most unjust; but to call even this an insult would be an act of folly, betokening, as I think, an unsound and unmanly habit of mind. Again, to call the unseen councillors of the Pope myrmidons, to speak of "aiders and abettors of the Papal chair," to call Rome "headquarters," these and like phrases amount, according to Archbishop Manning,* to "an indulgence of unchastened language rarely to be equalled." I frankly own that this is in my eyes irrational. Not that it is agreeable to me to employ even this far from immoderate liberty of controversial language. I would rather pay an unbroken reverence to all ministers of religion, and especially to one who fills the greatest See of Christendom. But I see this great personage, under ill advice, aiming heavy and, as far as he can make them so, deadly blows at the freedom of mankind, and therein not only at the structure of society, but at the very constitution of our nature, and the high designs of Providence for trying and training it. I cannot under the restraints of courtly phrase convey any adequate idea of such tremendous mischiefs; for, in proportion as the power is venerable, the abuse of it is pernicious. I am driven to the conclusion that this sensitiveness is at the best but morbid. The cause of it may be, that for the last thirty years, in this country at least, Ultramontanism has been very busy in making controversial war upon other people, with singularly little restraint of language; and has had far too little of the truth told to itself. Hence it has lost the habit, almost the idea, of equal laws in discussion. Of that system as a system, especially after the further review of it which it has been my duty to make, I must say that its influence is adverse

---

* Archbishop Manning, p. 177.

to freedom in the State, the family, and the individual; that when weak it is too often crafty, and when strong tyrannical; and that, though in this country no one could fairly deny to its professors the credit of doing what they think is for the glory of God, they exhibit in a notable degree the vast self-deluding forces, which make sport of our common nature. The great instrument to which they look for the promotion of Christianity seems to be an unmeasured exaltation of the clerical class and of its power, as against all that is secular and lay, an exaltation not less unhealthy for that order itself than for society at large. There are those who think, without being mere worshippers of Luther, that he saved the Church of Rome by alarming it, when its Popes, Cardinals, and Prelates were carrying it " down a steep place into the sea ;" and it may be that those who, even if too roughly, challenge the proceedings of the Vatican, are better promoting its interests than such as court its favours, and hang upon its lips.

I am concerned, however, to say that in the quick resentment which has been directed against clearness and strength of language, I seem to perceive not simply a natural sensitiveness, but a great deal of controversial stratagem. The purpose of my pamphlet was to show that the directors of the Roman Church had in the Council of the Vatican committed a gross offence against civil authority, and against civil freedom. The aim of most of those, who have professionally replied to me, seems to have been at all hazards to establish it in the minds of their flocks, that whatever is said against their high clerical superiors is said against them, although they had nothing to do with the Decrees, or with the choice or appointment of the exalted persons, who framed and passed them. But this proposition, if stated calmly as part of an argument, will not bear a moment's examination. Consequently, it has been boldly held that this drawing of distinctions between pastors and the flock, because the one made the Decrees and the other did not, is an insult and an outrage to all alike;* and by this appeal passion is stirred up to darken counsel, and obscure the case.

I am aware that this is no slight matter, and I have acted under a sense of no trivial responsibility. Rarely in the complicated combinations of politics, when holding a high place in the councils of my Sovereign, and when error was commonly visited by some form of sharp and speedy retribution, have I felt that sense as keenly. At any rate, I may and must say that all the words of these Tracts were written as by one who knows that he must answer for them to a Power higher than that of public opinion.

If any motive connected with religion helped to sway me, it was not one of hostility, but the reverse. My hostility, at least, was the sentiment which we feel towards faults which mar the excellencies, which even destroy the hope and the promise of those we are fain to love. Attached to my own religious communion, the Church of my birth and my country, I have never loved it with a merely sectional or insular attachment, but have thankfully regarded it as that portion of the great redeemed Christian family in which my lot had been cast—not by, but for me. In every other portion of that family, whatever its name, whatever its extent, whatever its perfections, or whatever

---

* I withhold the references—they are numerous, although by no means universal. Having said so much of the extreme doctrines of Archbishop Manning, I have pleasure in observing that he does not adopt this language. And also in acknowledging the charitable tone of Cardinal Cullen, who, in his Lenten Pastoral, commends me to the prayers of his people for my enlightenment.

its imperfections, I have sought to feel a kindly interest, varying in its degree according to the likeness it seemed to bear to the heavenly pattern, and according to the capacity it seemed to possess to minister to the health and welfare of the whole.

> "Le frondi, onde s' infronda tutto l' orto
> Del Ortolano Eterno, am' io cotanto
> Quanto da Lui in lor di bene è porto."*

Whether they be Tyrian or Trojan,† Eastern or Western, Reformed or Unreformed, I desire to renounce and repudiate all which needlessly wounds them, which does them less than justice, which overlooks their place in the affections and the care of the Everlasting Father of us all. Common sense seems to me to teach that doctrine, no less than Christianity. Therefore I will say, and I trust to the spirit of Charity to interpret me, I have always entertained a warm desire that the better elements might prevail over the worse in that great Latin communion which we call the Church of Rome, and which comprises one-half, or near one-half, of Christendom: for the Church which gave us Thomas à Kempis, and which produced the scholarlike and statesmanlike mind of Erasmus, the varied and attractive excellencies of Colet, and of More; for the Church of Pascal and Arnauld, of Nicole and Quesnel; for the Church of some now living among us, of whom none would deny that they are as humble, as tender, as self-renouncing, and as self-abased—in a word, as Evangelical as the most 'Evangelical' of Protestants by possibility can be.

---

* Dante, 'Paradiso,' xxvi. 64—6.
   "The leaves, wherewith embowered is all the garden
   Of the Eternal Gardener, do I love
   As much as He has granted them of good."—*Longfellow.*
† Æn. x. 108.

CONCLUSION.

No impartial student of history can, I think, fail to regard with much respect and some sympathy the body of British Christians which, from the middle period of the reign of Elizabeth down to the earlier portion of the present century, adhered with self-denying fidelity, and with a remarkable consistency of temper and belief, to the Latin communion. I lament its formation, and I cannot admit its title-deeds; but justice requires me to appreciate the high qualities which it has exhibited and sadly prolonged under sore disadvantage. It was small, and dispersed through a mass far from friendly. It was cut off from the ancient national hierarchy, and the noble establishments of the national religion: it was severely smitten by the penal laws, and its reasonable aspirations for the measures that would have secured relief were mercilessly thwarted and stifled by those Popes whom they loved too well. Amidst all these cruel difficulties, it retained within itself these high characteristics; it was moderate; it was brave; it was devout; it was learned; it was loyal.

In discussing, however sharply, the Vatican Decrees, I have endeavoured to keep faith; and I think that honour as well as prudence required me, when offering an appeal upon public and civil grounds, to abstain not only from assailing, but even from questioning in any manner or regard, the Roman Catholic religion, such as it stood before 1870 in its general theory, and such as it actually lived and breathed in England during my own early days, half a century ago.

It was to those members of such a body, who still cherish its traditions in consistency as well as in good faith, that I could alone, with any hope of profit, address my appeal. Who are they now? and how many? Has what was most noble in them gone the way of all flesh, together with those clergy of 1826 in England and Ireland, who, as Dr. Newman tells us, had been educated in Gallican opinions?

More than thirty years ago, I expressed to a near friend, slightly younger than myself, and in all gifts standing high even among the highest of his day, the deep alarm I had conceived at the probable consequences of those secessions of educated, able, devout, and in some instances most eminent men to the Church of Rome, which had then begun in series, and which continued for about ten years. I had then an apprehension, which after-experience has confirmed in my mind, though to some it may appear a paradox, that nothing would operate so powerfully upon the England of the nineteenth century as a crowd of these secessions—especially if from Oxford—in stimulating, strengthening, and extending the negative or destructive spirit in religion. My friend replied to me, that at any rate there would, if the case occurred, be some compensation in the powerful effect which any great English infusion could not fail to have, in softening the spirit, and modifying the general attitude, of the Church of Rome itself. The secessions continued, and multiplied. Some years later, the author of this remark himself plunged into the flood of them. How strangely and how sadly has his estimate of their effects been falsified! They are now seen, and felt as well as seen, to have contributed everywhere to the progress and to the highest exaggerations of Vaticanism, and to have altered in that sense both profoundly and extensively, and by a process which gives no sign of having even now reached its last stage, the complexion of the Anglo-Roman communion.

It is hard to recognise the traditions of such a body in the character and action of the Ultramontane policy, or in its influence either upon moderation, or upon learning, or upon loyalty, or upon the general peace.

I have above hazarded an opinion that in this country it may cause inconvenience; and I have had materials ready to hand which would, I think, have enabled me amply to prove this assertion. But to enter into these details might inflame the dispute, and I do not see that it is absolutely necessary. My object has been to produce, if possible, a temper of greater watchfulness; to promote the early and provident fear which, says Mr. Burke, is the mother of necessity; to disturb that lazy way of thought, which acknowledges no danger until it thunders at the doors; to warn my countrymen against the velvet paw, and smooth and soft exterior of a system which is dangerous to the foundations of civil order, and which any one of us may at any time encounter in his daily path. If I am challenged, I must not refuse to say it is not less dangerous, in its ultimate operation on the human mind, to the foundations of that Christian belief, which it loads with false excrescences, and strains even to the bursting.

In some of the works, to which I am now offering my rejoinder, a protest is raised against this discussion in the name of Peace.* I will not speak of the kind of peace which the Roman Propaganda has for the last thirty years been carrying through the private homes of England. But I look out into the world; and I find that now, and in great part since the Vatican Decrees, the Church of Rome, through the Court of Rome and its Head, the Pope, is in direct feud with Portugal, with Spain, with Germany, with Switzerland, with Austria, with Russia, with Brazil, with most of South America: in short, with the far larger

* Dr. Capel, p. 48. Archbishop Manning, p. 127.

part of Christendom. The particulars may be found in, nay, they almost fill, the Speeches, Letters, Allocutions, of the Pope himself. So notorious are the facts that, according to Archbishop Manning, they are due to a conspiracy of the Governments. He might as reasonably say they were due to the Council of the Amphictyons. On one point I must strongly insist. In my Expostulation, I laid stress upon the charge of an intention, on the part of Vaticanism, to promote the restoration of the temporal sovereignty of the Pope, on the first favourable opportunity, by foreign arms, and without reference to the wishes of those who were once his people. From Archbishop Manning downwards, not so much as one of those, who have answered me from his standing-ground, has disavowed this project: many of them have openly professed that they adopt it, and glory in it. The meaning of Monsignor Nardi, in his courteous Reply, written almost from beneath the Papal roof, cannot be mistaken (pp. 57–62). Thus my main practical accusation is admitted; and the main motive which prompted me is justified. I am afraid that the cry for peace, in the quarters from which it comes, has been the complaint of the foeman scaling the walls, against the sentry who gives the alarm. That alarm every man is entitled to give, when the very subject, that precipitates the discussion, is the performance of duties towards the Crown and State, to which we are all bound in common, and in which the common interest is so close, that their non-performance by any one is an injury to all the rest.

It may be true that in human things there are great restraining and equalising powers, which work unseen. It may be true that the men of good systems are worse than their principles, and the men of bad systems better than their principles. But, speaking of systems, and not of men, I am convinced that the time has come when religion itself requires a vigorous protest against this kind of religionism.

I am not one of those who find or imagine a hopeless hostility between authority and reason; or who undervalue the vital moment of Christianity to mankind. I believe that religion to be the determining condition of our well or ill-being, and its Church to have been and to be, in its several organisms, by far the greatest institution that the world has ever seen. The poles on which the dispensation rests are truth and freedom. Between this there is a holy, a divine union; and, he that impairs or impugns either, is alike the enemy of both. To tear, or to beguile away from man the attribute of inward liberty, is not only idle, I would almost say it is impious. When the Christian scheme first went forth, with all its authority, to regenerate the world, it did not discourage, but invited the free action of the human reason and the individual conscience, while it supplied these agents from within with the rules and motives of a humble, which was also a noble, self-restraint. The propagation of the Gospel was committed to an organized society; but in the constitution of that society, as we learn alike from Scripture and from history, the rights of all its orders were well distributed and guaranteed. Of these early provisions for a balance of Church-power, and for securing the laity against sacerdotal domination, the rigid conservatism of the Eastern Church presents us, even down to the present day, with an authentic and living record. But in the Churches subject to the Pope, clerical power, and every doctrine and usage favourable to clerical power, have been developed, and developed, and developed, while all that nurtured freedom, and all that guaranteed it, have been harassed and denounced, cabined and confined, attenuated and starved, with fits and starts of intermitted success and failure, but with a progress on the whole as decisively onward toward its aim, as that which some enthusiasts think they see in the natural movement of humanity at large. At last came the crowning stroke of 1870 : the legal extinction of Right, and the enthronement of Will in its place, throughout the Churches of one-half of Christendom. While freedom and its guarantees are thus attacked on one side, a multitude of busy but undisciplined and incoherent assailants, on the other, are making war, some upon Revelation, some upon dogma, some upon Theism itself. Far be it from me to question the integrity of either party. But as freedom can never be effectually established by the adversaries of that Gospel which has first made it a reality for all orders and degrees of men, so the Gospel never can be effectually defended by a policy, which declines to acknowledge the high place assigned to Liberty in the counsels of Providence, and which, upon the pretext of the abuse that like every other good she suffers, expels her from its system. Among the many noble thoughts of Homer, there is not one more noble or more penetrating than his judgment upon slavery. "On the day," he says, " that makes a bondman of the free,"

"Wide-seeing Zeus takes half the man away."

He thus judges, not because the slavery of his time was cruel, for evidently it was not; but because it was slavery. What he said against servitude in the social order, we may plead against Vaticanism in the spiritual sphere; and no cloud of incense, which zeal, or flattery, or even love, can raise, should hide the disastrous truth from the vision of mankind.

APPENDICES.

APPENDIX A (p. 5).

The following are the principal Replies from antagonists which I have seen. I have read the whole of them with care; and I have not knowingly omitted in this Rejoinder anything material to the main arguments that they contain. I place them as nearly as I can in chronological order :—

1. 'Reply to Mr. Gladstone.' By A Monk of St. Augustine's, Ramsgate. Nov. 15, 1874. London.
2. 'Expostulation *in extremis*.' By Lord Robert Montagu. London, 1874.
3. 'The Döllingerites, Mr. Gladstone, and the Apostates from the Faith.' By Bishop Ullathorne. Nov. 17, 1874. London.
4. 'The Abomination of Desolation.' By Rev. J. Coleridge, S.J. Nov. 23, 1874. London.
5. Very Rev. Canon Oakeley, Letters of. Nov. 16 and 27, 1874. In the 'Times.'
6. 'Catholic Allegiance.' By Bishop Clifford. Clifton, Nov. 25, 1874.
7. 'Pastoral Letters.' By Bishop Vaughan. Dec. 3, 1874. London. The same, with Appendices, Jan. 1875.
8. Review of Mr. Gladstone's Expostulation, in 'The Month' for Dec. 1874 and Jan. 1875. By Rev. T. B. Parkinson, S.J.
9. 'External Aspects of the Gladstone Controversy.' In 'The Month' of Jan. 1875.
10. 'An Ultramontane's Reply to Mr. Gladstone's Expostulations.' London, 1874.
11. Letter to J. D. Hutchinson, Esq. By Mr. J. Stores Smith, Nov. 29, 1874. In the 'Halifax Courier' of Dec. 5, 1874.
12. 'Letter to the Right Hon. W. E. Gladstone, M.P.' By A Scottish Catholic Layman. London, 1874.
13. 'Reply to the Right Hon. W. E. Gladstone's Political Expostulation.' By Monsignor Capel. London, 1874.
14. 'A Vindication of the Pope and the Catholic Religion.' By Mulhallen Marum, LL.B. Kilkenny, 1874.

15. 'Catholicity, Liberty, Allegiance, a Disquisition on Mr. Gladstone's Expostulation.' By Rev. John Curry, Jan. 1, 1875. London, Dublin, Bradford.
16. 'Mr. Gladstone's Expostulation Unravelled.' By Bishop Ullathorne. London, 1875.
17. 'Sul Tentativo Anticattolico in Inghilterra, e l'Opuscolo del On$^{mo.}$ Sig. Gladstone.' Di Monsignor Francesco Nardi. Roma, 1875.
18. 'A Letter to his Grace the Duke of Norfolk, on occasion of Mr. Gladstone's recent Expostulation.' By John Henry Newman, D.D., of the Oratory. London, 1875.
19. 'The Vatican Decrees in their bearing on Civil Allegiance.' By Henry Edward, Archbishop of Westminster. London, 1875.
20. 'The Dublin Review, Art. VII.' London, Jan. 1875.
21. 'The Union Review,' Art. I. By Mr. A. P. de Lisle. London, February, 1875.

I need not here refer particularly to the significant letters of favourable response which have proceeded from within the Roman Catholic communion, or from those who have been driven out of it by the Vatican Decrees.

APPENDIX B (p. 9).

" I lament not only to read the name, but to trace the arguments of Dr. Von Döllinger in the pamphlet before me."—*Abp. Manning. Letter to the 'Times,' Nov. 7, 1874.—'Vatican Decrees,'* p. 4.

Justice to Dr. Von Döllinger requires me to state that he had no concern, direct or indirect, in the production or the publication of the tract, and that he was, until it had gone to press, ignorant of its existence. Had he been a party to it, it could not have failed to be far more worthy of the attention it received.

Bishop Ullathorne goes further, and says of Dr. Von Döllinger that " he never was a theologian."—*Letter*, p. 10.

Then they have made strange mistakes in Germany.

Werner, a writer who I believe is trustworthy, in his 'Geschichte der Katholischen Theologie,' 1866, is led by his subject to survey the actual staff and condition of the Roman Church. He says, p. 470: "Almost for an entire generation, Dr. I. Von Döllinger has been held *the most learned theologian of Catholic Germany;* and he indisputably counts among the greatest intellectual lights that the Catholic Church of the present age has to show."

I cite a still higher authority in Cardinal Schwarzenberg, Archbishop of Prague. On May 25, 1868, he addressed a letter to Cardinal Antonelli, in which he pointed out that the theologians, who had been summoned from Germany to the Council, were all of the same theological school, and that for the treatment of dogmatic matters it was most important that some more profound students, of more rich and universal learning, as well as sound in faith, should be called. He goes on to suggest the names of Hefele, Kuhn, and (with a high eulogy) Von Döllinger.

The strangest of all is yet behind. Cardinal Antonelli, in his reply dated July 15, receives with some favour the suggestion of Cardinal Schwarzenberg, and says that one of the three theologians named would certainly have been invited to the Council, had not the Pope been informed that if invited, he would decline to come. That one was Dr. Von Döllinger.

I cite the original documents, which will be found in Friedrich's 'Documenta ad illustrandum Conc. Vat.,' pp. 277-80.

APPENDIX C (p. 26).

As I have cited Schrader elsewhere, I cite him here also; simply because he translates (into German) upon a different construction of the Seventy-third Article of the Syllabus from that which I had adopted, and makes a disjunctive proposition out of two statements which appear to be in effect identical. In English, his conversion of the article runs as follows:—

"Among Christians no true matrimony can be constituted by virtue of a civil contract; and it is true that either the marriage contract between Christians is a Sacrament, or that the contract is null when the Sacrament is excluded.

"Remark. And, on this very account, is every contract entered into between man and woman, among Christians, without the Sacrament, in virtue of any civil law whatever, nothing else than a shameful and pernicious concubinage, so strongly condemned by the Church; and therefore the marriage-bond can never be separated from the Sacrament."*

The sum of the matter seems to be this. Wherever it has

---

* Schrader, Heft ii. p. 79. Wien, 1865.

pleased the Pope to proclaim the Tridentine Decrees, civil marriage is concubinage. It is the duty of each concubinary (or party to concubinage), with or without the consent of the other party, to quit that guilty state. And as no law of Church or State binds a concubinary to marriage with the other concubinary, he (or she) is free, so far as the Church of Rome can create the freedom, to marry another person.

APPENDIX D (p. 51).

I do not think myself called upon to reply to the statements by which Bishop Vaughan has sought ('Pastoral Letter,' pp. 35-7) to show, that the fear of civil war ultimately turned the scale in the minds of the chief Ministers of 1829, and led them to propose the Bill for Emancipation. First, because the question is not what influences acted at that moment on those particular minds, but how that equilibrium of moral forces in the country had been brought about which made civil war, or something that might be called civil war, a possibility. Secondly, because I am content with the reply provided in the *Concio* of Archbishop Kenrick, c. viii. See Friedrich's 'Documenta ad illustrandum Concilium Vaticanum,' vol. i. p. 219. The statements would, in truth, only be relevant, if they were meant to show that the Roman Catholics of that day were justified in making false statements of their belief in order to obtain civil equality, but that, as those statements did not avail to conciliate the Ministers of 1829, they then materially fell back upon the true ones.

To show, however, how long a time had to pass before the poison could obtain possession of the body, I point, without comment, to the subjoined statement, anonymous, but, so far as I know, uncontradicted, and given with minute particulars, which would have made the exposure of falsehood perfectly easy. It is taken from the 'Cornish Telegraph' of Dec. 9, 1874, and is signed Clericus. It follows a corresponding statement with regard to America, which is completely corroborated by Archbishop Kenrick in his *Concio*: see Friedrich's 'Documenta,' i. 215.

"Of a painful alteration in another popular work, Keenan's 'Controversial Catechism,' (London, Catholic Publishing and Bookselling Company, 53, New Bond Street,) I can speak from two gravely differing copies, both professedly of the same edition, now lying before me. This is so singular a case that I venture to give it in a little detail. Keenan's 'Catechism' has been very extensively used in Great Britain and America. In his preface to the third edition, the author speaks of it as 'having the high approbation of Archbishop Hughes, the Right Rev. Drs. Kyle and Carruthers; as well as the approval of the Right Rev. Dr. Gillis, and the Right Rev. Dr. Murdoch.' These last-named four ecclesiastics were vicars-apostolic of their respective districts in Scotland, and their separate episcopal approbations are prefixed to the 'Catechism;' those of Bishops Carruthers and Kyle are dated, respectively, 10th and 15th April, 1846; those of Bishops Gillis and Murdoch, 14th and 19th November, 1853.

"Thus this work was authenticated by a well-known American archbishop and four British bishops thoroughly familiar with the teaching of their Church, long before Archbishop Manning joined it. Now, at page 112 of one of my copies of the 'new edition, corrected by the author, twenty-fourth thousand,' are the following question and answer:—

Q.—"'Must not Catholics believe the Pope in himself to be infallible?'

"*A.*—'This is a Protestant invention; it is no article of the Catholic faith; no decision of his can oblige, under pain of heresy, unless it be received and enforced by the teaching body,—that is, by the bishops of the Church.'

"It would be satisfactory if Archbishop Manning would explain how his statement to Mr. Bennett squares with this statement of Keenan's, and with that of the 50 *Reasons.*

"But, further, it would be highly satisfactory if Archbishop Manning, or some representative of the 'Catholic Publishing and Bookselling Company' would explain how it came to pass that, on the passing of the Vatican decree, apparently whilst this very edition of Keenan's *Catechism* was passing through the press, the above crucial question and answer were quietly dropped out, though no intimation whatsoever was given that this vital alteration was made in the remainder of the edition. Had a note been appended, intimating that this change had become needful, no objection, of course, could have been made. But no word has been inserted to announce, or explain, this omission of so material a passage; whilst the utmost pains have been taken, and, I must add, with great success, to pass off this gravely altered book as being identical with the rest of the edition. The title-pages of both copies alike profess that it is the 'new edition, corrected by the author,' (who was in his grave before the Vatican Council was dreamed of); both profess to be of the 'twenty-fourth thousand;' both have the same episcopal approbations and prefaces; both are paged alike throughout; so that, from title-page to index, both copies are, apparently, identical. I have very often placed both in the hands of friends, and asked if they could detect any difference, but have always found they did not. The Roman Catholic booksellers, Messrs. Kelly and Messrs. Gill, in Dublin, from whom I purchased a number of copies in August, 1871, were equally unaware of this change; both believed that the Publishing Company had supplied them with the same book, and both expressed strongly their surprise at finding the change made without notice. Another Dublin Roman Catholic bookseller was very indignant at this imposition, and strongly urged me to expose it. It is no accidental slip of the press; for whilst all the earliest copies of the edition I bought from Messrs. Kelly contained the question and answer, they were omitted in all the later copies of Messrs. Gill's supply. The omission is very neatly, cleverly made by a slight widening of the spaces between the questions and answers on page 112 and the beginning of page 113; so skilfully managed that nobody would be at all likely to notice the difference in these pages of the two copies, unless he carefully looked, as I did, for the express purpose of seeing if both alike contained this question and answer."

APPENDIX E (p. 51).

Extract from 'The Catholic Question;' addressed to the Freeholders of the County of York, on the General Election of 1826, p. 31.

"The Catholic religion has three great æras; first in its commencement to the dark ages; then from the middle centuries down to the Reformation; and lastly from the Reformation to the present day. The Popish religion of the present day has scarcely any resemblance with its middle stage; its powers, its pretensions, its doctrines, its wealth and its object are not the same; it is a phantom, both in theory and practice, to what it once was; and yet the bigots draw all their arguments from the Middle Ages and, passing all the manifest alterations of modern times, set up a cry about the enormities of times long past, and which have been dead and buried these three hundred years. This unjust conduct is just the same as if you were to hang a faithful, tried domestic, who had served you forty years, because he had committed some petty theft when he was a boy. It is the most illiberal and the most unjustifiable mode of arguing, and if applied to the Church of England, would reduce it to a worse case than that of her old rival."

The "bigots," who are here charged by the Liberal electors of Yorkshire with reviving mediæval Romanism, are not Vaticanists, but Protestant bigots, whose sinister predictions the Vaticanists have done, and are doing, their best to verify.

Both by reason of the language of this extract, and of its being taken out of the actual working armoury of one of the great electioneering struggles for the County of York, which then much predominated in importance over every other constituency of the United Kingdom, it is important. It shows by direct evidence how the mitigated professions of the day told, and justly told, on the popular mind of England.

APPENDIX F (p. 59).

I. From the Decree.

"Et primò declarat, quod ipsa in Spiritu Sancto legitimè congregata, concilium generale faciens, et ecclesiam Catholicam repræsentans, potestatem a Christo immediatè habet, cui quilibet cujusque status vel dignitatis, etiam si papalis existat, obedire tenetur *in his quæ pertinent ad fidem* et extirpationem dicti schismatis, et reformationem dictæ ecclesiæ in capite et in membris."— Conc. Const. Sess. v.; Labbe et Cossart, tom. xii. p. 22.

From the account of the Pope's confirmation.

"Quibus sic factis, sanctissimus dominus noster papa dixit, respondendo ad prædicta, quod omnia et singula determinata conclusa et decreta *in materiis fidei* per præsens concilium, conciliariter tenore et inviolabiliter observare volebat, et nunquam contraire quoquo modo. Ipsaque sic conciliariter facta approbat et ratificat, et non aliter, nec alio modo."—Conc. Const. Sess. xlv.; Labbe et Cossart, tom. xii. p. 258.

APPENDIX G (p. 68).

Labbe, Concilia, x. 1127, ed. Paris, 1671, Canon II.

"*Obedite præpositis vestris, et subjacete illis; ipsi enim prævigilant pro animabus vestris, tanquam rationem reddituri:* Paulus magnus Apostolus præcepit. Itaque beatissimum Papam Nicolaum tanquam organum Sancti Spiritus habentes,* necnon et sanctissimum Hadrianum Papam, successorem ejus, definimus atque sancimus, etiam omnia quæ ab eis synodicè per diversa tempora exposita sunt et promulgata, *tam pro defensione ac statu Constantinopolitanorum ecclesiæ, et summi sacerdotis ejus, Ignatii videlicet, sanctissimi Patriarchæ, quam etiam pro Photii, neophyti et invasoris,* expulsione ac condemnatione, *servari semper et custodiri cum expositis capitulis immutilata pariter et illæsa.*"

The Canon then goes on to enact penalties.

APPENDIX H (p. 76).

It appears to me that Archbishop Manning has completely misapprehended the history of the settlement of Maryland and the establishment of toleration there for all believers in the Holy Trinity. It was a wise measure, for which the two Lords Baltimore, father and son, deserve the highest honour. But the measure was really defensive; and its main and very legitimate purpose [plainly was to secure the free exercise of the Roman Catholic religion. Immigration into the colony was by the Charter free: and only by this and other popular provisions could the territory have been extricated from the grasp of its neighbours in Virginia who claimed it as their own. It was apprehended that the Puritans would flood it, as they did: and it seems certain that but for this excellent provision, the handful of Roman Catholic founders would have been unable to hold their ground. The facts are given in Bancroft's 'History of the United States,' vol. i. chap. vii.

I feel it necessary, in concluding this answer, to state that Archbishop Manning has fallen into most serious inaccuracy in his letter of November 10 (p. 6), where he describes my Expostulation as the first event which has overcast a friendship of forty-five years. I allude to the subject with regret; and without entering into details.

---

* In the Greek, *ibid.* p. 1167, ὡς ὄργανον τοῦ ἁγίου Πνεύματος ἔχοντες.

www.ingramcontent.com/pod-product-compliance
Lightning Source LLC
Chambersburg PA
CBHW021918180426
43199CB00032B/524